BASIC ILLUSTRATED

Camping

BASIC ILLUSTRATED

Camping

Second Edition

Cliff Jacobson

Illustrations by Lon Levin

FALCONGUIDES

GUILFORD, CONNECTICUT
HELENA, MONTANA

FALCONGUIDES®

An imprint of Rowman & Littlefield
Falcon, FalconGuides, and Outfit Your Mind are registered trademarks of Rowman & Littlefield.

Distributed by NATIONAL BOOK NETWORK
Copyright © 2015 by Cliff Jacobson

Illustrations by Lon Levin
Photos by Cliff Jacobson unless otherwise noted.

British Library Cataloguing in Publication Information Available

Library of Congress Cataloging-in-Publication Data

Jacobson, Cliff.
  Basic illustrated. Camping / Cliff Jacobson ; illustrations by Lon Levin. — second edition
      pages cm
  Includes index.
  ISBN 978-1-4930-1253-4 (pbk.) — ISBN 978-1-4930-1915-1 (ebook) 1. Camping. I. Levin, Lon, ill.
II. Title. III. Title: Camping.
  GV191.7.J327 2015
  796.54—dc23
                                                                            2015017364

The author and Globe Pequot assume no liability for accidents happening to, or injuries sustained by, readers who engage in the activities described in this book.

Contents

Acknowledgments

A special thanks to Dr. Bill Forgey and Tom Todd, who at the start, believed in the idea of this book. To my editor, Katie Benoit Cardoso, who pressed for a revised edition. And to my friends Rob Kesselring (RobKesselring.com), David Morlock (morlockphotography.com), and Steve Piragis of Piragis Northwoods Company (piragis.com), for photos they graciously provided.

Introduction

I discovered the joys of camping at the age of twelve in a rustic Scout camp set deep in the Michigan woods. It was 1952, just before the dawn of nylon tents and 60/40 parkas. Aluminum canoes were hot off the Grumman forms, though I'd never seen one. Deep down, I believed they'd never replace the glorious Old Towns and Thompsons.

Like most kids my age, I had little money for outdoor gear. What I earned by picking pop bottles off the roadway went for a secondhand bike or a Randolph Scott movie. My camping outfit was carefully assembled from a ragtag assortment of military surplus and Salvation Army store items. I knew only one kid who had equipment that was new. Once I saved enough to buy an official Boy Scout knife, which in those days came with good carbon steel blades and a metal BSA insignia.

One Christmas Dad gave me an all-steel Scout handaxe, which came complete with tooled leather sheath and varnished wood scales. For twenty years thereafter I proudly carried it on all my hiking and canoe trips. It was my edge for making fires on a rainy day. Early on, I decided that those who bad-mouthed hatchets simply lacked the skills to use them right. I still retain that conviction, as you'll see in Chapter 2.

On my fourteenth birthday I received another treasured gift—a solid brass M 71 Primus stove, which, at five dollars, was a genuinely expensive gift.

These items, along with an army surplus wool sleeping bag and poncho, comprised my store of camping items. Everything fit nicely into a tan canvas packsack and together tipped the scale at barely 20 pounds. To this, add a week's worth of dehydrated Seidel trail foods, a handful of big stick matches, and a spartan change of clothes, and I was ready for the great adventure.

At last I owned all the tripping gear I'd ever need. What boy could be more fortunate? Admittedly, I yearned for an army down-and-feathers sleeping bag—the wool one I had was adequate only in the heat of summer. But no matter: With an extra blanket and knitted sweater, I got by. Even in snow. After all, being a little cold was part of the camping game, wasn't it?

My bible on how to camp was the *Boy Scout Handbook*, which, I was told, contained absolutely everything one could want to know about the great outdoors. It was all there—from how to trench a tent and build a bed of pine boughs to the construction of rope-lashed furniture and emergency dwellings. Axmanship was serious stuff, so it was treated as a separate chapter.

Environmental concerns? There were none. Not that we didn't care, you understand. We just didn't see anything wrong with cutting trees and restructuring the soil to suit our needs. Given the equipment of the day, reshaping the land was the most logical way to make outdoor life bearable.

Litter, of course, was another matter. We proudly packed out everything we (and anyone else) brought in. We were Boy Scouts, not slobs!

In 1958 Calvin Rutstrum brought out his first book, *The Way of the Wilderness*. Suddenly, there was new philosophy afield. Calvin knew the days of trenched tents and bough beds were numbered. His writings challenged readers to think before they cut, to use an air mattress instead of a spruce bed. Wilderness camping was in proud transition. New products—nylon, Dacron, stainless steel, and vinyl—were already fragmenting the monopolies enjoyed by cotton, wool, and canvas. Outfitters by the thousands sold (or burned) their cotton tents and joined the nylon revolution.

Suddenly the emphasis had shifted from skills to things. Knowing how was no longer good enough. Everyone needed a plethora of new gear— down sleeping bags and foam sleeping pads; Swiss Army knives with a tool for everything; waterproof boots with Vibram lugs; two-piece rain suits with clever hoods that moved with the turn of a head; polypropylene socks and underwear and fleece pullovers; Erector-set tents that needed no staking; Gore-Tex suits that breathed in the rain; color-matched designer clothes that looked good at the All-Stars game; and tiny trail stoves that ran on canisters of liquid butane.

Suddenly I felt quite inadequate, like a peasant in Camelot.

Calvin Rutstrum summed it up one foggy morning on a mid-September day. I'd driven up to meet him at his wilderness cabin on the North shore of Lake Superior. Cal had built the place himself, every inch of it. No need to pour a concrete slab; a mirror-flat shelf of slate was good enough. The double cabin was artfully constructed from native pine. And it was solid!

As Cal poured coffee, I baited him by pulling from its stuff sack a polyester-filled sleeping bag I'd purchased for my wife.

"Whatcha think of these new poly bags?" I asked. "They dry really fast— could be a lifesaver if you get your down bag wet."

With that, Rutstrum, in his early eighties, slammed down his cup on the wood-pinned table and splashed brown liquid onto the varnished wood. Slowly he rose, his set jaw and steel gray eyes poised in anger.

"Damn!" he called loudly: "I've canoed and camped for nigh on seventy years and I've never gotten my down bag wet. Never. Not ever! Those who get stuff wet on a trip need help. They need to learn how to camp!"

I could have cheered!

It seems as though high-tech gear and high-powered salesmanship have become a substitute for rock-solid camping skills. Chemical fire-starters take the place of correct fire making; indestructible canoes are the solution to hitting rocks; blizzard-proof tents become the answer to one's inability to stormproof conventional designs. And the what-if-you-get-your-down-bag-wet syndrome attracts new converts each year. In the end only the manufacturers win. For even the best gear falls short of expectations without proper know-how.

And that, friends, is what this book is all about. No pressure to buy the new, discard the old. Just a mash of proven procedures to enhance your camping trips.

How to Use This Guide

This guide covers all the basics you need to know before you go camping, from selecting gear to building a fire. To ensure that you make the most of every outing, this book also includes tips for dealing with common camping problems. There are luscious recipes and slick tricks for managing meals on miserable days, ways to stormproof the popular self-supporting dome tents, and tips for rigging tarps in big winds. The recommended procedures you should follow when confronted by a bear—and when protecting your food from one—have changed considerably in recent years. So you'll want to read this section carefully before your next campout.

There's ammunition to help you win your battle with bugs and bad weather as well as tips for sleeping soundly on rough ground. Check out the chapter on the dangers of camping out.

If you like what you read and want to learn even more about the topics covered in this book, look for my other books: *Camping's Top Secrets, 25*th *Anniversary Edition, Basic Illustrated ® Cooking in the Outdoors, Basic Illustrated ® Map and Compass,* and *Basic Illustrated ® Knots for the Outdoors.*

I'm proud of this revision. It's chock-full of all the important things you really need to know to enjoy camping out.

CHAPTER 1

How to Use Your Gear Effectively

I once checked the contents of a popular backpacking book and found that around 90 percent of its pages were devoted to the selection of equipment. There were full chapters on Choosing the Sleeping Bag, A Tent for All Seasons, and Getting Booted Up. Except for some obvious advice about pitching camp on high ground and packing clothes in waterproof bags, there was precious little of value to crow about. Right then, I vowed to take a more practical tack in this book.

Certainly, proper equipment is important to a quality outdoor experience. Only a fool would suggest otherwise. But the engineering specifics of every product are available free from the manufacturer, and detailed equipment evaluations are the annual rule in almost every outdoor magazine. And if you're still confused over what variables go into selecting a great tent or sleeping bag, just ask the folks who sell outdoor gear at first-rate camping shops. Most of these young men and women are quite knowledgeable, and just about all are active hikers, bikers, canoeists, and skiers. High-tech camping equipment is not usually sold on commission, which means the purveyors will react honestly to your concerns.

So rather than clutter this chapter with equipment trivia that is readily available elsewhere, I'll suggest some ways to make your good gear perform at its best.

Sleeping Bags

Selecting Your Sleeping Bag

What you choose depends on how classy you want to travel and how much you want to spend. At the top of the list are three-hundred dollar down bags, while at the bottom are twenty-nine dollar astro-fill specials that are no better than paired blankets. And speaking of blankets: a set of airy acrylic or loose-woven wool blankets, sandwiched á la Boy Scout style (Figure 1-1), makes a perfectly good bed for typical summer campouts. If cost is an object, here's the place to cut: There's no sense buying three-season protection if you'll use it only in the blistering heat of summer. Most campers own bags that are too warm. Only if you're heading to the far north should you consider the merits of an autumn-rated (25-degree Fahrenheit) sleeping bag. For car camping (which really can't be called sleeping out), any sleeping bag will do. Other-wise, my vote goes to a roomy mummy bag with a fully formed head and boxed (raised) foot. Be sure the bag has a two-way zipper that runs from foot to chin.

In sleeping bags, more than any other camping product, you get exactly what you pay for. At this writing, $125 will put you into a quality synthetic bag. Twice this will buy a good down bag.

So which one is for you? First, be aware that good down will outlast the best Polarguard/Hollofil/Quallofil by decades. Conscientious bag makers sug-gest a useful life of around five years for a heavily used synthetic bag. With down bags, the nylon shell goes first. How long? Well, one of my down bags is nearly forty years old, and it's still going strong!

As to the argument that down bags are hard to dry when they get wet on a camping trip, rethink the logic of Calvin Rutstrum. If you pack your bag as I suggest, you'll never get it wet. Not ever!

Figure 1-1
For summer use, blankets will work as well as a sleeping bag. Here's how to fold them for maximum warmth.

Most people choose sleeping bags that are too warm. For summer camping, a bag rated to 35 degrees F is warm enough. For three-season camping, a 20 degree rated bag will do. For snow camping, place two summer weight bags inside one another. Generally, mummy bags, with their built-in hoods are lighter, warmer and more compact than rectangular shaped sleeping bags (which don't have hoods). **Tip:** *If you're a cold sleeper, wear light wool or synthetic (no cotton!) long underwear to bed. The long johns will add 10 degrees or more of warmth to your sleeping system.*

     Water-resistant down sleeping bags. New on the scene are sleeping bags whose down is chemically treated to resist water. Whereas conventional down bags will absorb significant amounts of moisture from the air, DriDown™ bags retain nearly all of their loft (and warmth) regardless of temperature and humidity. If the down does get wet, it will dry much faster than untreated down. My take? In all my years of canoeing and camping, I've never gotten my down bag wet. Still, for camping in prolonged rain or snow, a DriDown™ bag may be the smart way to go.

Packing Your Sleeping Bag

The recommended procedure for waterproofing the sleeping bag is to stuff it into a nylon sack that has first been lined with a plastic bag. This is foolish advice! Every time you stuff the bag into the plastic sack, you stretch and abrade the plastic. In no time, tears—and leaks—develop. Some experts know this and so suggest that you carry some extra plastic bags, which is even more absurd.

     Here's a better way: First, stuff the bag into its nylon sack (which need not be watertight), then set the sack inside a sturdy plastic bag. Pleat and twist the end of the plastic bag, fold it over and secure it with a loop of shock-cord. Then, place this unit into an oversize nylon sack (again, which need not be waterproof). Note that the delicate plastic liner—which is the only real water barrier—is protected from abrasion on both sides!

It's especially important to adopt this procedure if you'll be tying your sleeping bag onto the outside of a pack frame, where it will be constantly exposed to the weather. You'll also appreciate the extra abrasion resistance of the sandwiched construction when you hike through thorns or brambles. On one occasion I sliced through an outer stuff sack while hiking in rough country.

In camp. Some authorities advise you to lay out your sleeping bag and fluff it to full loft well in advance of bedtime. This is supposed to increase its insulative value. Hogwash! Better to leave the bag stuffed and protected until you need it. A good sleeping bag will fluff to full loft within a minute after it's pulled from the sack. Just give it a good shake before you climb in.

Washing Your Sleeping Bag

A good sleeping bag may last a lifetime if it is aired frequently and stored properly. Washing—by hand or machine—should be done only when absolutely necessary. Sleeping bags lose loft and, therefore, warmth, with every washing. The baffles take a beating too. Rough handling—by machine or you—can destroy the bag. Dry-cleaning is a dangerous option; the cleaning fluids will strip the oils from down and maybe melt synthetic fill. And solvents retained by the insulation may make you sick! In the end, your bag will be clean but it may not be safe or warm. Washing, by hand or machine is the only way to go.

Things you'll need:

- Specialty detergents for cleaning down and synthetic sleeping bags are highly recommended. But any mild soap, like Ivory Snow or Woolite, works fine if you rinse it completely. Do not use harsh laundry detergents!
- Some old cotton bath towels and a few tennis balls (optional).
- A bathtub (if you hand-wash) or a large-capacity, front-loading washing machine. Do not use a top-loader; the agitating motion can tear the baffles.

Machine washing:

1. Use warm water, gentle cycle. Rinse and spin twice.
2. If your laundromat has a high-speed water "extractor," use it after the final spin cycle. Otherwise, proceed to step 3.

3. Place the bag in a commercial clothes dryer, set to the *lowest* temperature. Toss in some heavy cotton towels to absorb water and some tennis balls (optional) to break up clumps. Caution: Many dryers put out too much heat, even on their lowest setting. Open the door and bleed heat every few minutes, or run the dryer with the door slightly ajar—a rolled magazine jammed between the door hinge and power button will keep it running. If the dryer stops, restart it immediately. Don't let the bag rest against the hot drum! Be sure the bag is *completely* dry before you store it.

Hand washing:

The bathtub is your washing machine. Allow the bag to sit in the suds for an hour or more. Every few minutes, press down with your hands to gently work soap into the fill. Don't wring or twist the bag. Rinse twice with clear water to be sure you get all the soap out. Press down to remove as much water as possible, then fully support the bag as you transfer it to a netted hammock or chaise lounge. Air-drying may take many days. Machine drying is safer and faster.

Trail Mattresses

A mattress will smooth the way for old bones and warm your backside when you sleep on cold ground. There are four basic types of trail mattresses.

Air mattress. Except for car camping, the traditional air mattress is extinct. Except in the heat of summer, air mattresses cannot be used with down sleeping bags. Body weight compresses an air mattress down to near-zero thickness (synthetics are less affected): If the ground is cold, your backside is, too! If you want to be comfortable and warm, place a thin, closed-cell foam pad on top of your air mattress.

Closed-cell foam. Closed-cell foam insulates efficiently and is waterproof, inexpensive, and unaffected by punctures . . . and not very comfortable. It's the foam of choice for subzero camping, however, where a mattress failure could be serious. Three-eighths of an inch is thick enough for summer: double that for use on snow. It is the best pad for children, especially those who may wet their beds.

Fabric-covered open-cell foam. This is basically a huge sponge covered with nylon or cotton. This design is reasonably comfortable, inexpensive, unaffected by punctures, and not waterproof. Open-cell foam is bulky when rolled, and it doesn't insulate as well as closed-cell foam.

Air-filled foam pads. The Therma-Rest began the revolution; now there's lots of competition. Basically, these units consist of a low-density (soft and cushy) open-cell foam that's sealed in an envelope of vinyl and nylon. An oversized plastic valve controls the air flow. Open the valve and the pad inflates itself. Close the valve to lock in the air. The resulting mattress is very comfortable, incredibly warm, and surprisingly reliable.

New on the scene are ***air-mattresses that are insulated with goose down or synthetics.*** These are as warm as air-filled foam pads but they're thicker and more comfortable on rough ground. The Exped SynMat 9 and NEMO Cosmo insulated pads are two of my favorites. They have built-in pumps and inflate in less than a minute. Deflation is almost instantaneous. Important: Avoid any pad that is slow to inflate or deflate—it will wear you out.

Some Trail Mattress Tips

Make a tough cotton or light wool cover for your air-filled foam pad. The cover will protect the pad from punctures and keep it from sliding on the slippery nylon tent floor. In hot weather the cotton or wool material will be more comfortable to sleep on than the nonporous nylon shell of the air pad.

Don't use a cotton cover in winter: Damp cotton will draw heat from your body. Winter covers should be made from pure polyester or tightly woven wool.

A crinkly "space blanket" (every discount store has them), set silver side up under your foam pad, will add considerable warmth to your sleeping system.

If you find yourself sleeping on an uncomfortable incline, level out your sleeping system by placing folded clothes beneath your air mat or foam pad.

Choose a mattress that inflates and deflates fast. It's obvious that this camper is not having a good time!

This method can make an otherwise intolerable sleeping situation quite bearable.

Tip. If you are stuck with an inclined site, pitch your tent perpendicular to the drop (one side lower than the other), rather than parallel to it with the entrance high, as suggested in most camping books. It's easier to level a "sunken side" than a "lowered end."

Figure 1-2
Sleeping comfortably on an incline.

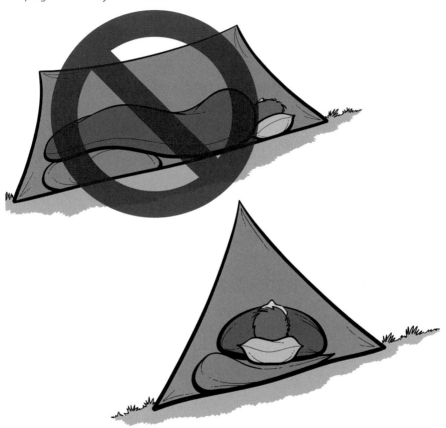

Tents

You don't need a sophisticated high-altitude tent for general camping. Any simple forest tent will do if it has a bathtub floor (no perimeter seams at ground level) and a waterproof fly that stakes nearly to the ground. The fly must cover every seam and floor corner. If you rely on glue (seam sealant) to waterproof exposed seams, you're just asking for trouble. A vestibule (alcove) is important: It provides a place to store equipment out of the weather. Vestibules also seal the entryway of a tent from blowing rain and snow.

The rainfly on this Eureka! Tundraline tent stakes right to the ground (rain can't blow in). Note the spacious vestibules. A camp along the Rio Grande River, Texas.

Each person needs about 2½ by 7 feet just to stretch out. Add an additional half foot (3 feet x 7½ feet) plus headroom enough to dress, and you enter the realm of comfort. A tent used for general camping should be relatively commodious—a 6-foot by 8-foot floor plan (commonly referred to as a three-to-four-person tent) is ideal for two. Weight? Under twelve pounds, and the lighter the better. Serious backpackers will opt for the lightest, most compact tent they can get, which may or may not be a good idea. If you have to spend the day weather-bound in a doghousy little shelter with no room to sit upright, you'll wish you'd brought a bigger tent. Your tent is your home away from home, so this is not the place to cut corners.

You'll pay much more for high-tech geometrics (domes, tunnels, and such) than for simple-to-sew but reliable A-frames. If you're going to the mountains and need the reliability of a windproof tent, by all means get one. But if your camping will be confined to the tree line, choose a more moderate design—one that enables you to keep your sanity in an all-day rain.

Don't leave home without installing a plastic groundcloth inside your tent. The groundsheet will prevent pooled surface water, which wicks through floor seams (and in time, worn floor fabric), from entering your sleeping area. Don't place the plastic sheet under the tent as advised by some tent-makers—rain water may become trapped between it and the floor and be

This tent was swamped by heavy rain. In the adjacent photo, note how an interior groundsheet saved the day!

Make the groundsheet larger than the tent floor. It should flow at least 6 inches up the sidewalls, all around. Water that gets into your tent will be trapped under the plastic and you'll stay dry!

pressure-wicked (from body weight) through the nylon fabric into the tent. You'll really have a sponge party if this happens! Use of an interior ground-cloth is the best wet-weather tip I can give you. On numerous occasions, this feature has saved me from an unexpected midnight bath.

Almost any tent can be made to survive a severe storm, if you know how to rig it. Chapter 6 shows you how.

Tent Poles, Stakes, and Cords

Tent poles should be made of aluminum, never of fiberglass or plastic, which can break. Wands (not supporting members), which are used to hold out awnings and vents, are an exception. All poles should be shock-corded for easy assembly.

Some Tent Pole Tips

Tent poles won't jam together and will slide more easily through pole sleeves if you polish the joints (a one-time effort) with 400-grit wet sandpaper and then wipe them with a cloth sprayed with liquid silicone.

To release pole sections that are stuck together, heat the joint lightly in the flame of your trail stove. The joint will expand and the poles will part easily.

Bring a variety of tent stakes. L to R: 12-inch arrow-shaft stakes (soft ground), aluminum pins (rocky ground), U-pound 'em tri-corner stakes (very hard ground). Note the variety of cords.

Tent stakes. Twelve-inch-long arrow-shaft aluminum stakes or "staples" (u-shaped stakes) hold best in sand; sharp aluminum skewers are good for compacted soil; and narrow steel wire stakes are ideal for rocky ground. Carry a variety of tent stakes so you'll always have what works best.

Tip. 8-inch-long aluminum concrete nails make acceptable low-cost tent stakes. The heavy steel-and-plastic "U-pound 'em" stakes sold at discount stores are useful only on big, semi-permanent canvas tents.

Special stakes are unnecessary for camping on snow or sand. Conventional aluminum stakes can be buried, or guylines wound about wooden sticks, then buried. Tin can lids (with the edges peened in for safety) make good snow stakes. Run the guylines through holes in the center and bury the lids.

Cords. You can never have too much cord on a camping trip. I bring about 200 feet of parachute cord, cut into 10 to 15 foot lengths. If you learn the "sheet bend" on page 69, you will be able to daisy-chain cords together when you need more length. **Tip.** Yellow, glow-in-the-dark cords are easier to see in dim light than white parachute cords.

Hammocks

When I was a boy scout in the 1950s, I owned a military surplus jungle hammock. It had a waterproof fly and zippered bug net. Unlike a tent, my hammock never blew down or leaked in rain. I much preferred it to the tiny pup tents of the day. For years, I mourned the passing of that hammock and hoped

Hammocks are back! Note the large rainfly that is pitched over this Eagles Nest Outfitters (ENO) hammock. Boundary Waters Canoe Area, Minnesota.

a manufacturer would bring it back. Well, hammocks are here again, and they are more popular than ever! Some models even have detachable rain flies and bug screens. They are made of strong nylon and come in cool colors.

Clothing and Rain Gear

You don't need outdoor designer wear to enjoy camping. Simply avoid wearing cotton, except in the height of summer heat, and you'll do fine. Blue jeans are a particularly bad choice: Once they get wet and cold, they stay that way. A number of deaths due to hypothermia (see Chapter 8) have been traced to the wearing of this article.

A lot of very experienced campers do all their shopping at army surplus and discount stores, where they find good-quality items at low prices. Military woolens, inexpensive acrylics, and polyester fleece are the favored regimen, as are cotton/polyester and cotton/nylon fatigues.

A breathable nylon jacket is essential to stem the biting winds, and don't forget polypropylene, polyester, or wool long johns when the need arises. Be aware that polypropylene absorbs body odors and smells awful after a few days on the trail. Polyesters are much better. My wife, Sue Harings, is more conscious of odors than I am, and she insists that I recommend Thermax™ and its relative Thermostat by name. Terramar body-sensors™ are also quite odor-free over the long haul.

Don't thumb your nose at traditional wool garments. Unlike synthetics, tightly woven wool resists sparks and wind and will repel a substantial rain, and it's not dissolved by harsh chemicals (such as insect repellents). Wool also keeps you warm when it's soaked with water (synthetics may need to be wrung out). Despite all the hoopla about synthetics, pure virgin wool remains the strongest, most reliable fiber you can wear in mean weather. Super soft, non-scratching woolens (merino) are available. Some names to remember are: Icebreaker®, Smartwool®, Woolpower (Klar® Ullfrotte), Ibex, Woolrich, and Filson.

Taking along one change of clothes from nose to toes is the rule, whether you're going for a weekend or a month. Everything should fit easily into an 8-inch by 12-inch nylon stuff sack.

Rain gear should be uncomplicated. A two-piece rain suit is better than a poncho, which dribbles through, or a knee-length shirt (cagoule), which is awkward for everything except lazing about camp. The best buys on rainwear are usually found in industrial supply stores where construction workers shop. The new construction-grade rain suits are strong, light, and wondrously inexpensive. They'll keep you plenty dry, even though they lack the exquisite

A rain suit offers better protection than a poncho or knee-length rain shirt. Author (left) is wearing Chota® Hippies—ultralight waterproof/breathable hip waders. The tent is a Hilliberg Kaitum (tunnel design). A campsite along the Kopka River, Ontario, Canada.

tailoring, multiple pockets, and exotic hoods (which you really don't need) of high-tech camp store garments.

Waterproof-breathable garments. Gore-tex™ started the "waterproof-breathable" revolution; now, there are many competitors—each touting advantages. Be aware that waterproof-breathable garments don't eliminate perspiration as rapidly as those made from uncoated (porous) cotton, nylon or Dacron—important if you work hard and sweat a lot. **Note:** Gore-Tex fabrics *must* be kept clean for top performance. Use liquid detergents only, unless the hang-tag says otherwise.

Important! Do not wear your rain gear for wind protection, as is commonly advised. Any item that is frequently worn will eventually develop holes. Wear your nylon shell jacket for wind and keep the Gore-tex or polycoated stuff for its intended purpose. Always store rain clothes in a nylon sack to eliminate the abrasion that results from stuffing these garments into packsacks.

What you wear under rain gear is important. A light polypropylene or wool shirt will eliminate the clammy feeling that results from wearing waterproof clothing next to the skin.

So you're taking the children. No sense spending a bundle on clothing that will be outgrown in a season. Acrylics are the key. They are very inexpensive and dry almost instantly after a rain. A light, non-allergenic acrylic sweater worn next to the skin makes a fine underwear top for chilly weather. Again, avoid blue jeans: Cotton/polyester slacks dry faster and are cheaper. Rain gear is easy: A cut-down plastic poncho worn over a waterproof nylon jacket (double protection plus dry sleeves) will keep a youngster dry in the worst storms. Add a plastic souwester hat and rubber boots, and your little one is set for a delightful day afield.

Footwear

The trend is to very lightweight boots for all but the most demanding applications. No knowledgeable hiker I know would be caught dead wearing the five-pound Vibram lug monstrosities that were so popular decades ago. Now footwear rules are simple: Wear the lightest, most flexible boot you can find. Exceptions are mountaineering and winter travel. Two friends recently completed a trek from Nukla, Nepal, to the Base Camp of Mount Everest—a distance of about 40 miles, all uphill, on rocky yak trails and across snow fields. They wore lightweight fabric walking shoes (recommended by their guide) and merino wool socks. They had no foot problems at all.

Even the best shoes become uncomfortable after a long day afield. Always bring a second pair of shoes (Crocs, tennis, or moccasins) for camp.

Proper footwear is important. Generally, the lighter the boots, the better. Even the best boots become uncomfortable after a long day afield. Always bring a second pair of comfortable shoes (Crocs®, tennies, or moccasins) for camp.

Socks

Socks should be nearly pure wool or a wicking synthetic. Cotton absorbs perspiration and encourages blisters. Some hikers wear one pair of heavy socks; others prefer two—a medium-weight wool outer pair and lightweight wool or polypropylene liners. The liners are generally worn inside-out to keep abrasive seams away from the skin. This eliminates hot spots and blisters. This was my preference until a few years ago when I discovered that one pair of FITS socks (fitssocks.com) were enough. FITS socks are seamless and made from soft merino wool. They don't chafe, ride up, or stretch out-of-shape even when they're worn for many days. They are quite extraordinary!

Packs

What you need depends entirely on your tripping style. For backpacking on relatively good trails, the aluminum-frame outfit reigns supreme. Rock scrambling requires more dexterity; hence, the development of the "soft pack" with internal stays. And for canoeing, nothing beats the venerable Duluth pack (Figure 1-3), which is nothing more than a canvas envelope with three closing straps. There are also a number of specialized packsacks designed for technical rock climbing and day meandering.

A hard pack is useful for storing items that might gouge your back. L to R: 5-gallon pail with spin-on waterproof Gamma Seal® lid; Cooke Custom Sewing (CCS) quad-pocket barrel pack (accepts the pail at left); CCS foam-lined food pack (insulates food); E.M. Wanigan box (no longer manufactured), 60 Liter barrel with harness; Number 2 Duluth "Cruiser" pack with an Adirondack pack basket inside).

Figure 1-3

The Duluth pack, a canvas envelope that measures 24 by 30 inches, is the preferred pack for canoeing.

A hard pack (plastic box, ice chest, olive barrel, foam-lined pack) is handy for storing hard items like stoves and cookware that may gouge your back. Hard packs will protect your food from rain, mice, and squirrels but they WON'T discourage bears (see "Bears", page 57).

How to pack your pack. Now that most packs come with internal or external frames, the science of proper packing has all but vanished. And that's too bad, because there is an efficient way to do things.

Proper packing begins with effective waterproofing. Now write this in Technicolor: Regardless of the manufacturer's claims, my pack is not waterproof! Even double-coated pack fabrics are not foolproof. After all, there are seams. And fabrics do wear. The slightest scratch will allow a leak.

So start by lining your pack with a large plastic bag. Inside this, place a light fabric abrasion liner of some sort. The liner need not be waterproof—sheer polypropylene or nylon taffeta will do. Its only purpose is to absorb the abrasion that results from stuffing gear deep into the pack. The sandwich principle is the same as that recommended for packing the sleeping bag.

Exterior pack pockets must also be waterproofed. Ziplock bags are one solution; the pack rain coat—a tailored poly-coated nylon apron which fits over the pack—is another. In camp, a giant plastic garbage bag can be used to protect everything from rain.

Principles of packing. Pack in <u>horizontal</u>, not vertical, layers. Why? Because your pack should follow the spinal curve of your back. An unyielding upright (tent pole, rolled sleeping pad, etc.) spoils the S-curve. Packing will go easier if you place loose items in stuff sacks. Sacks that reach wall-to-wall across your pack will maximize pack space and eliminate small gaps that are hard to fill.

Generally, you should pack in the <u>reverse order</u> you'll need things—food on the bottom, tent on top, etc. <u>Exceptions</u>: Place heavier items near the top (keeps weight closer to your back) when hiking groomed trails. Set heavy things close to the bottom for better control when bushwhacking.

Packing the tent. Here's your most obstinate load: Invariably the poles will be too long to fit in the pack. Most hikers respond by simply setting the lengthy tent bag under the closing flap of their packsack, which is hardly a good idea for these reasons: 1) It raises the load too high, which may unbalance the hiker; 2) the tent is exposed to the elements and thorny vegetation; 3) rain can get into the pack by working its way under the badly sealed closing flap.

Far better to pack tent and poles separately as follows:

1.   Stuff (my preference) or roll the tent, without stakes and poles, and place it in an oversize nylon bag. Pack poles and stakes in a separate nylon bag with drawstring closure.

2.   Pack the tent between the waterproof plastic pack liner and the tightly rolled fabric abrasion liner. This will isolate (the possibly damp or wet tent) from the dry gear below. Set the pole and stake bag on top of the tent bag and cinch down the flap. If the poles are longer than the pack is wide, run the closing straps of the pack flap through loops of nylon cord sewn to the ends of the pole bag as shown in Figure 1-4.

3.   Cinch the pack flap down tightly. The nylon cords keep the pole bag from sliding out beneath the pack flap.

Figure 1-4
Pack the tent and poles separately. Set the pole and stake bag just under the pack flap and run the closing straps of the pack flap through loops of nylon cord sewn to the ends of the pole bag.

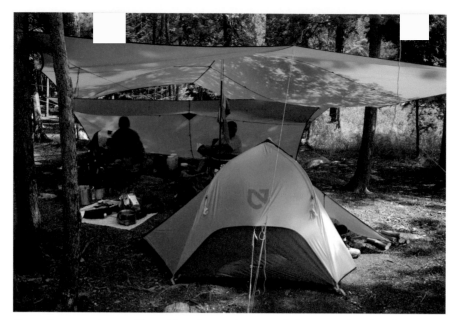

One or two nylon tarps, will provide a dry, wind-protected place to cook and gather. Boundary Waters Canoe Area, Minnesota.

Rain Fly (Tarp)

One or two nylon rain tarps, tightly pitched between trees, will enable you to prepare meals, make repairs, and otherwise enjoy a rainy day. The rain tarp is one of the most essential and overlooked items on a camping trip. Chapter 6 provides an in-depth look at how to rig it.

Stove

A stove is essential in all but the most unfrequented areas. I prefer the self-contained single-burner gasoline models, though the small two-burner Colemans are your best buy. The stove is so important, I've allotted a full chapter to it.

Lighting Devices

For most types of tent camping, a small, LED head lamp is all you need. Bring a more powerful "focused" light if you're camping with teenagers. I once canoed for hours around a huge lake in the black of night—mini-flashlight in my mouth—in search of two kids who had gone fishing.

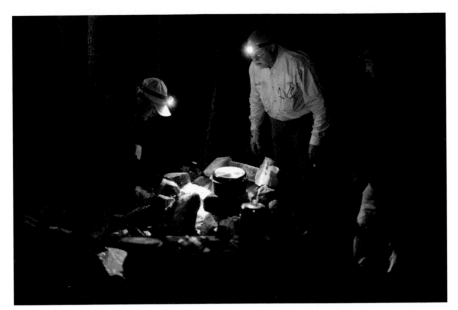

Headlamps have all but replaced flashlights. Boundary Waters Canoe Area, Minnesota.   Dave Morlock

In 2004, I had a dicey bear encounter in Saskatchewan. The sky was dark gray when this bad boy came into camp. We tried to shoo him away, but he just kept coming. One man activated his SureFire tactical light (the size of a Magic Marker), which really lit up the bush. In a flash the bear was gone.

Tactical lights are so bright that they will momentarily blind an attacker—perhaps even a bear!

Tools

Just about anything can be fixed in the field if you have the right tools.

For predictable outings, a Swiss Army knife, duct tape, and nylon parachute cord are enough. Add a pair of pliers with a cutting edge and you're set for most emergencies.

For an ultra-compact kit, I recommend the Leatherman "Wave" multitool. With it, you can field-strip eyeglasses, fishing reels, and your gasoline stove. There's a file, scissors, an assortment of screwdrivers, and more. The saw blade cuts through hardened aluminum—handy if you have to repair a broken tent pole.

Tip. Beware of any nylon tool sheath that has a Velcro closure.

A marine-grade snap (easy to install) is more much more reliable, especially if you hike through thick brush or take a tumble in the woods.

Folding Camp Stool

Camp chores—cooking, washing dishes, etc.—go easier when you don't have to sit on the ground. I've tried all manner of stool designs and have ultimately settled on a simple, collapsible model that sits on two parallel aluminum rails. Avoid individual pointed legs that can sink into soft ground. My favorite stool has a canvas storage pouch beneath the seat. When not in use, it folds flat and attaches (with bungee cords) to my backpack.

A folding stool adds to your comfort. My favorite chair (left) has horizontal legs that won't sink into the ground. It folds flat and can be secured to the face of a pack with a bungee cord and carabiners. **Tip:** *When it's cold, I place a piece of closed cell foam on the seat of my stool. Available from Piragis Northwoods Co. (piragis.com).*

The author's favorite stool—secured to a pack.

CHAPTER 2

The Cutting Edge

In the 1920s there were the sheath knife and full-size axe. By 1950 the common jackknife and three-quarter-length axe were in style. The 1970s brought forth the red-handled Swiss Army knife. In the 1980s lock-back knives were popular; now the trend is to serrated tactical knives (which are generally useless for camping) and multipurpose tools like the Leatherman and Gerber multipliers, and no axe at all.

Somewhere in their vacillation, campers have overlooked an important fact: Slicing cheese, splitting kindling, and other knife-related chores are about the same today as a century ago. It follows then that your choice of edged tools should—with appropriate modifications—reflect these similarities.

The primary use of a camp knife is to prepare food and kindling. The blade should be thin for effortless slicing and long enough to reach to the bottom of the peanut butter jar.

Here's my formula for a camp knife:

1. Enough length (4- to 5-inch blade) to slice meat and cheese and to reach deep into the peanut butter jar without getting all gunked up.

2. A thin, flat-ground blade for effortless slicing. Nearly all knives sold for outdoor use have blades that are too thick. One-eighth inch across the spine is the maximum thickness permissible for a utility knife, no matter how delicate the edge. Try slicing a tomato with the typical hunting knife and you'll see why.

The primary camp knife may be a fixed blade or folding model. You'll pay more for a good folder than for a sheath knife of similar length. A fixed blade is best if you will use the knife to split kindling, as shown on page 25.

If your taste runs to folding knives, select a model with a 3- to 4-inch-long, thin, flat-ground blade. If you want a razor-sharp edge that's easy to maintain, choose carbon steel over stainless. Invariably, you'll need two knives for camping—a thin-ground kitchen-style model for preparing foods and a substantial multipurpose folder of some sort.

Some of the author's favorite knives. Top to bottom: Idaho Knife Works, "Cliff" knife/author's design; Mora Kniv (they come from the factory, shaving sharp!); Spyderco Military Knife (this one is left-handed); Victorinox "Forester"(locking blade). The sheath knives are carbon steel; the folders are stainless. Note the author's handmade left-handed sheath. Plans for making sheaths like this can be found in Camping's Top Secrets, 25th Anniversary Edition.

Sharpening. Never use an electrical sharpener or one of those mechanical wheeled gadgets sold at supermarkets. You'll ruin the knife beyond repair! Instead, get a synthetic diamond stone (first choice) and/or a medium-grit soft Arkansas stone. If you want the finest razor edge, obtain a hard Arkansas stone as well. If the blade is nicked or extremely dull, you may want to start with a coarse carborundum stone which you can buy at any hardware store. Seriously deep nicks may be removed with a file.

Maintain a light film of cutting oil, WD-40 or transmission oil, on the natural stones (use water on diamond stones) to float away steel particles. Carborundum stones can be used dry or with water or oil. Just don't mix lubricants. Raise the back of the blade 10 to 20 degrees and cut into the stone, as illustrated.

Clean the stone and blade frequently and apply new oil during the sharpening process. I generally take four strokes per side and apply new oil (first, cleaning off the old) every thirty strokes or so. When sharpening is complete, I strop the blade on leather to produce a razor-fine edge.

Maintain a 10–20 degree angle and cut into the stone. Use oil or WD-40 on natural stones; water only on diamond stones.

The Hand Axe

It's almost impossible to maintain a bright fire after a weeklong rain without a wood-splitting tool of some sort. A big axe is fine if weight is no object and you've got the space to carry it. Otherwise, a high-quality hand axe will do. Gransfors of Sweden (gransfors.com) makes the very best. Despite what you may have heard about the dangers of hatchets, they are quite safe if you follow the "splitting" guidelines in Figure 2-1. When used with a folding saw, a hand axe will produce all the camp wood you need with very little effort.

Three of the author's favorite axes. Front to back: *Gransfors mini-hatchet (ultra light—ideal for solo camping); Gransfors Wildlife Hatchet (a good choice for small groups); Gransfors Small Forest axe (best for large groups and remote camping).*

Figure 2-1
Splitting wood is easy if you use the axe as a splitting wedge rather than a "chopping" tool. Thick logs can be split by this method.

Figure 2-2
Kindling splits easier from the end grain—a process that is made easier (and safer) if you use a stick of wood to hold the upright piece in place.

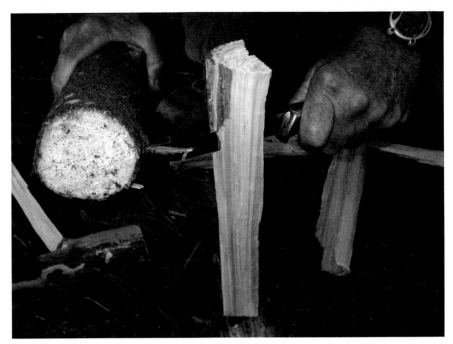

A sheath knife can be used to split smaller logs and kindling.

Warning! Do not pound on the spine of a folding knife, even one with a locking blade—you may damage the spring and the blade could close on your hand!

To avoid *ax*idents, follow these rules:

1. Saw wood to be split into 12-inch lengths.

2. Use the hand axe as a splitting wedge: Do not chop with it! The folding saw performs all cutting functions.

3. Set the axe head lightly into the end grain of the wood (Figure 2-1). One person holds the tool while a friend pounds it through with a chunk of log. When splitting very thick (more than 6 inches thick) logs, take multiple splittings off the edges.

   Caution. Hold the axe solidly with both hands. Allow the log hammer to do all the work.

   To produce kindling. Kindling splits easiest from the end grain, a process that's made easier and safer if you use a stick of wood to hold the upright in place (Figure 2-2).

   Sharpening the axe. Remove nicks with a flat mill file. True the edge with a diamond stone or soft Arkansas stone. Leave a coating of oil on the blade to resist rust.

Folding Saw

This tool is a must for making fire on a rainy day. Steel-framed bow saws are sturdy (fine for car camping) but they don't pack well. Triangular-shaped aluminum-framed folding saws are flimsy, and their triangular shapes don't permit you to cut big logs. I prefer a full-frame wooden saw, like the Fast Bucksaw (fastbucksaw.com) pictured here. Regrettably, the excellent aluminum Sawvivor® saws recommended in previous editions of this book are no longer manufactured.

The author used this Gransfors mini-hatchet and folding Fast Bucksaw (fastbucksaw.com) to cut and split this wood. The "Littlbug" stove (littlbug.com) at right is the author's favorite woodburning stove. The new Agawacanyon (agawacanyoninc.com) Boreal 21 packsaw (not shown), is the most rigid and powerful aluminum-frame folding saw I've found. It assembles in seconds and quickly rips through thick logs.

CHAPTER 3

To Build a Fire

The ability to make fire when the woods are drenched from rain is one of the most difficult and important of all outdoor tasks. Yet it is a skill that few people possess. Here's how to get the job done quickly and efficiently, regardless of the whims of nature.

Some years ago, after a gentle rain, I watched for an hour while two teenagers tried to build a campfire. The boys struck match after match without success, ultimately giving up in disgust. I casually strolled over, rearranged a few pieces of wood, and with a single match, set the mass aflame.

After witnessing scores of similar episodes, I concluded that while anyone can make fire on a sun-scorched day, precious few have the ability when the weather deteriorates to persistent rain.

Skeptical? Stroll around a state park campground after a tingling thundershower and count the number of fires you see burning brightly compared to the amount of wet gear hanging hopelessly out to dry.

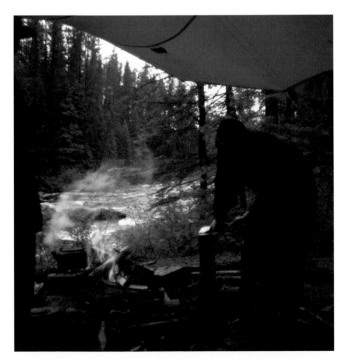

If you can make a fire on a rainy day—and with just one match—you'll be a hero to your friends. Along the Kopka River, Ontario, Canada.

Wilderness guidebooks suggest that a knowledgeable woodsman can start a fire with a single match instantly in a major storm. Hardly! No one can make fire reliably under these conditions, but anyone can succeed in a moderate downpour or weeklong drizzle if he or she knows how.

Know-how begins with the right tinder, and to come up with that, you'll need the right tools—a folding saw, a small hand axe (hatchet), and a sharp knife—hence the importance of the previous chapter.

Now for that tinder. In the north country, the tendency is to search for birchbark—much to the detriment of the birch trees and displeasure of campers who may later occupy the site. Besides, any birchbark you find during or immediately after a good soaking rain is probably too wet to burn anyway. And on a dry day there are better alternatives.

Instead, seek out the dead, pencil-thin branches near the base of evergreen trees. These shade-killed twigs are protected from rain by the tree canopy and are usually bone-dry. They'll break with a crisp snap even after days of prolonged rain. If the branches are wet to the touch but you can hear the snap, the wood's dry enough to burn. A handful of this tinder is all you need.

If evergreen twigs are rain-soaked or unavailable (and in state parks they are not available), locate a log with a dry center. Search the open areas of your campsite for a length of jutting birch, pine, cedar, or other softwood. When you find one of these "blowdowns" poking into the clearing, saw off a section that doesn't touch the ground. Touch the cut end to your cheek or lips. The outer sapwood may be damp, but the heartwood should feel dry. Some basic biology here: You'll find deadfalls in the woods as well as in the open, but they're often rotten from the dampness of the forest—and rotten wood, as everyone knows, burns poorly. However, snags that protrude from the forest are flooded with sunlight (which kills most decay-causing microorganisms) and so are more apt to have sound, dry wood inside.

Saw the sunlit section of log into 12-inch lengths and split and sliver it with the hand axe by the method outlined in Chapter 2.

Next, slice long thin slivers of wood from the heartwood splittings. This is your tinder. When you have plenty of tinder on hand, build your fire step-by-step.

Step One

Set two 1-inch-thick sticks parallel to one another about 6 inches apart. Place three pencil-thin pieces of kindling over them at right angles. Space the pieces of kindling about half-an-inch apart. Don't spread the tinder over a wide area. Keep the tinder box small—no larger than the lid of a small tin can (see top photo on next page).

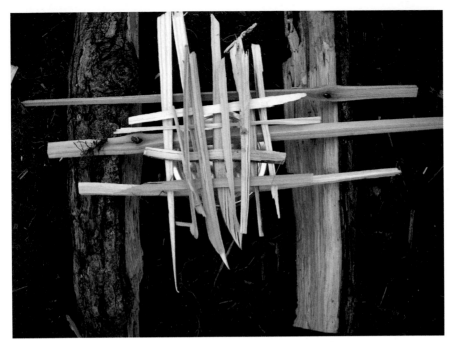

Place long, thin shavings (tinder) on top of the kindling. Space the shavings so you can see "light" between them. The tin can lid is just a reference to show the size of the fire box.

Bridge across the fire base with two thick sticks then set thin kindling on top. The kindling will hold the shavings in place and provide fuel for the developing flame.

The fire will start with a single match. Note the bright, smoke-free flame.

Step Two

Carefully place long, thin shavings or small, dry twigs (tinder) on top of the kindling. Don't crowd the tinder; the fire must have adequate ventilation to burn properly.

Next, put two sticks about ½-inch in diameter over the ends of the 1-inch-thick sticks at right angles to the fire base. These sticks will support the heavier kindling, which you will pile atop the shavings.

Step Three

When you've stacked the shavings about 1 inch high, weight them in place (so the wind won't blow them away) with several criss-crossed pencil-thin sticks. Follow this with a few larger pieces of wood. For best results, use split kindling rather than sticks gathered from the forest floor.

Your fire is now ready to light. It will start with a single match.

The procedure I've outlined is time-consuming but foolproof. The unique construction of the fire guarantees success because:

1. The match is applied directly below the tinder in keeping with the principle that heat (and flame) goes upward, not sideways. Typical campfires are ordinarily ignited along the edge.

2. The tinder box is elevated, which produces an efficient chimney-like draft. The rich, smoke-free flame of the young blaze gains momentum quickly.

3. The tinder doesn't touch the cold, damp ground.

Tips

In the piney woods of the North and East, look for the balsam fir tree. Its sap is nearly as volatile as kerosene. In summer the tree produces half-dollar-size resin blisters on its trunk. Lance a few blisters with a sharp stick and collect the pitch on a piece of wood or bark. Set the "resin cup" directly under your fire base and light it. Voilá! Fire every time—with one match.

Carry a butane lighter and save matches for emergencies. Also bring a candle plus some Mautz Fire Ribbon or other chemical fire-starter. Cotton balls dipped in Vaseline and cigar-sized logs made from rolled newspaper that are soaked in paraffin are good fire starters. For trips where a quick warming fire may be required, assemble these kit materials: A flattened half-gallon milk carton, a handful of thick shavings, and some splittings of scrap wood. Put everything into a nested pair of plastic bags.

When the emergency strikes, dump everything on the ground, frizz up the milk carton, and splash it with Fire Ribbon. Light the ribbon and toss all the wood on top. The carton will burn for about three minutes, the wood an additional five. That's enough time for you to search the woods for more fuel while your wet friend is being re-warmed by your instant blaze.

Let's review the rules for making a successful fire:

1. Place sticks far enough apart on the fire base so there'll be adequate ventilation for the developing flames. The most common reason for fire failure is lack of oxygen.

2. Tinder should be no larger in diameter than the thickness of a match. Trying to ignite wood larger than that on a damp day is a waste of time.

3. Don't heap the fire base high with wood during the developing stages of the flame. Unnecessary fuel just draws heat from the young fire and cools it. Preset pyramid-style fires (`a la Boy Scouts) look nice in handbooks but burn inefficiently. Once you complete Step 3, wood should be added one stick at a time and placed strategically so you can see light between each one. Smoke is nature's way of telling you you're suffocating the blaze.

   Banking the fire to preserve fuel. Use this procedure when you have a good, hot fire but little wood to maintain it. "Bank" your fire by setting small logs parallel to one another across the top. The rule of thumb for a smoke-free flame is to allow a radius width between parallel pieces of wood. Thus, a pair of 2-inch-thick logs should be separated by a full inch to ensure adequate ventilation. Banking will reduce this distance to a mere (though identifiable) slit, which will naturally diminish use of oxygen and slow combustion. You should also eliminate any breeze coming into the fire. A large, flat rock—don't get one from a lake or river because the moisture it contains may cause it to explode—or tier of logs works fine.

Tip. When the wood is really wet, a "tubular fire blower" can save the day. To make one, you'll need a 4-inch-long piece of narrow-diameter copper or aluminum tubing and about 18 inches of plastic or rubber "Bunsen-burner" hose. Most hardware stores have these materials. The "Fire Dragon"—a commercial fire-blower—is available from Piragis Northwoods Company (piragis.com).

Use your "blower" to nurse a fickle flame and whenever wood is too thick or damp to burn well. The concentrated air turbocharges hot coals and turns them into willing flames

Extinguishing the blaze. It should go without saying that your fire must be dead out when you leave your campsite. The rules are simple: When the smoke is gone and you have thoroughly doused everything with water, check the fire with your hands. If it's hot enough to burn your fingers, it's hot enough to burn a forest.

Using a Campfire Dragon (tubular fire-blower) to nurse a stubborn blaze. Boundary Waters Canoe Area, Minnesota. Piragis Northwoods Co.

CHAPTER 4

Choosing a Camp Stove

You can, of course, cook everything over an open fire. And a lot of campers do just that. But maintaining a cooking fire in the typical state park campground—where wood must be purchased at five dollars a bundle—is comparable to burning money. In the deep backcountry, a stove is less essential, for good wood is readily found. If, however, you've driven many miles to a favorite wilderness and found a fire ban in effect, you'll wish you'd brought a stove.

Summary of Stove Types

There are gasoline, kerosene, propane, butane, alcohol, and wood (twig)-burning stoves. There are also some "multifuel" stoves, which are purported to burn a number of different liquid fuels. These may not put out as much heat as those designed to burn white gas (naphtha) only.

Gasoline stoves are the most reliable of the pack, especially in bad weather. And gasoline has the highest heat output of all stove fuels. Generally, gasoline stoves accept only "white" gas or Coleman fuel (highly refined forms of naphtha). It's not safe to burn leaded gasoline in them. An important distinction must be made between additive-free white gasoline—which is difficult to obtain—and additive-packed automotive unleaded gasoline, which is available at every gas station. Unleaded gas is more volatile than white gas and may produce excessive pressures in stoves designed for white gas only.

Kerosene has about the same BTU rating as gasoline, but it's less volatile. Where a gasoline stove will explode, a kerosene stove will simply burn. But kerosene stoves are smelly, and they must be primed with alcohol or gasoline. Nonetheless, they are very safe and are grand for camp cooking.

Propane is relatively inexpensive and it puts out good heat. Its big drawback is in the packaging: The heavy steel cylinders that contain the gas are fine in a Vanbago but not in the packsack of a hiker or paddler.

Butane stoves need no priming, pumping, or filling. Refueling consists of snapping on a new gas cylinder. But these stoves are temperature-sensitive;

Two of the author's favorite stoves. Left: Primus Omnifuel (white gas)/windshield not shown. Note the extra long fuel delivery tube which keeps the tank well away from the burner. Right: Glowmaster (butane)—it lights instantly!

the colder the weather, the less heat they put out. And the longer they run, the cooler they burn. Models with fuel canisters that sit below the burner receive reflected heat from the pot above and are therefore less sensitive to this cooling phenomenon. Butane stoves are fine for high-altitude work where the gas develops sufficient pressure. But for all-around camping, there are better alternatives.

Blended fuels. Some manufacturers blend butane and propane for better cold-weather performance; however, their heat output is still well below that of stoves that burn white gas.

Alcohol stoves are safe, reliable and dead quiet. Just light the burner and you're ready to cook. Alcohol stoves are slow to heat, however. Most require ten to fifteen minutes to boil a quart of water! My favorite alcohol stove is the Swedish-designed Trangia Cooker, which is part stove, part "cooker." The Trangia was designed to run on alcohol (HEET in the yellow can works well) but it can also be fueled with butane or white gas if you have the optional accessories. The unit comes with an adjustable-damper alcohol burner, two nesting pots, a skillet and pot-lifter, and a tea kettle. The huge windscreen defies the strongest wind. It is compact and rugged.

The Trangia Cooker runs on alcohol (burner is left of stove). It's set up here to burn butane. Note the large, effective windscreen.

Sterno is a solid form of alcohol that comes in a can. Sterno puts out enough heat to warm food but not cook it.

Wood-burning stoves. Wood stoves are lightweight and powerful, and the twigs they burn are free. But the wood burns fast, so you'll have to keep fueling the stove as you cook. The exception—and my favorite—is the Littlbug (littlbug.com) stove shown on page 26, which accepts logs as thick as three inches! When cranked up, it puts out as much heat as a campfire. The Littlbug consists of two pieces of sheet metal (stainless steel) that snap together to form a chimney, similar to that used to ignite charcoal. It weighs 19 ounces, and when packed it takes up almost no space at all. If you camp where fires must be contained within a fire-pan, the Littlbug will qualify if you set it on a metal pan that meets government specifications (12" x 12" x 1.5"). A lightweight steel oil-drain pan or an aluminum pizza pan with minimum 1.5-inch sides will qualify. Both combos are lighter and more compact than the nine-pound-plus fire-pans provided by outfitters.

Stove Features

Stability. There's nothing more frustrating than simmering a big pot of spaghetti on a precarious little beast that wobbles with every stir of the spoon.

Before you buy, remember that some stoves that look great in the store tip over in the field.

Ease of starting. Butane and propane stoves start instantly. Gasoline and kerosene models require priming—some models flare violently until warmed. Fast, easy ignition is a plus for any stove.

Susceptibility to wind. The first time you have to build a rock wall around your stove to keep it perking you'll understand the value of a good windscreen.

Adjustable flame. If you intend to fry pancakes or simmer stew, you'll want an infinitely adjustable flame—a feature most gasoline trail stoves don't have. The venerable Coleman twin burner and compact PEAK 1 are exceptions. Propane and butane stoves all throttle down to a simmering whisper. Alcohol stoves have just one speed—full blast! The Trangia has a damper that allows some adjustment.

Plastic parts. Plastic is bad medicine for stove parts. Plastic hardens with heat and age and eventually breaks. If there's a stove flare-up, plastic will melt and burn. Also stay away from any stove that does not have a flameproof armored fuel line.

Here are some dos and don'ts that will keep your camp stove perking merrily season after season.

Dos

- Do carry fuel only in recommended containers. Volatiles are best transported in aluminum liter bottles or in the original steel can.

- Do frequently check the temperature of your stove's fuel tank by feeling it with your hand. If the tank is too hot to hold, reduce the stove's heat and/or pour cold water on the tank.

- Do always use a windscreen on stoves whose fuel tanks are connected to the burner with an armored hose.

- Do protect fuel line connectors from dirt and damage (cover them with a plastic bag or cap) when you pack your stove away.

- Do carry extra stove parts and tools. An extra pressure cap seal and pump washer are usually enough. Bring a small screwdriver and pliers. A dental tool is useful for removing O-rings and gaskets.

- Do empty the fuel in your stove after every trip. Impurities in fuel left in stoves can cause malfunctions. ***Note:*** This is the most common cause of long-term stove failure.

Don'ts

- Don't loosen or remove the filler cap of a gasoline stove when the stove is burning. This could result in an explosion.

- Don't refuel a hot stove. There may be sufficient heat still available to ignite the gas fumes.

- Don't set oversize pots on stoves that have integral fuel tanks. Large pots reflect excessive heat back to the fuel tank, which may cause overheating of the stove. Run stoves at three-fourths of maximum heat output if you use oversize pots.

- Don't use automotive gasoline (regular or unleaded) in a stove designed to burn white gas.

- Don't start a stove inside a tent or confined area; the resulting flare-up can be dangerous.

- Don't operate any stove without sufficient ventilation. A closed tent is not sufficiently ventilated.

- Don't set stoves on sleeping bags or tent floors. There's enough heat generated at the base of some stoves to melt or warp these items.

- Don't run stoves that have integral fuel tanks at full power for extended periods of time. The tank may overheat and cause the safety valve to blow. Stoves with separate fuel tanks that are connected with an armored fuel line can be run at full power indefinitely if their tanks are shielded with a reflector (windscreen).

- Don't enclose a stove with aluminum foil to increase its heat output. The stove may overheat and explode.

- Don't fill gasoline or kerosene stoves more than three-fourths full. Fuel won't vaporize if there's insufficient room for it to expand.

CHAPTER 5

Tasty Routes to Dining Out

There are two schools of thought about camp cooking: One prefers spending whatever time is required to make delicious meals, even if it means sweating for hours over a smoky fire and dutch oven. The other view goes something like this: "Since I spend only about a week a year in the outdoors, I like to keep foods simple. If it takes more than twenty minutes to prepare, forget it."

I prefer the latter approach, as the following example illustrates: Some years ago, after a gentle rain, I went for an evening paddle along the shore of a popular lake in the Boundary Waters Canoe Area. As I rounded a point, I happened upon a man and woman sitting contentedly on a rock ledge, staring into the starlit sky. I paddled over and struck up a conversation, in the course of which I asked: "How come you folks don't have a bright, cheery fire going?"

With this, the man began his story. He and his wife were newcomers to the backcountry—neither had canoed or camped before. They arranged to have an outfitter supply all their needs, and he reciprocated by providing a wealth of slow-cook foods. There were pancakes and French toast for breakfast, grilled cheese sandwiches and soup for lunch, and multicourse dried foods for supper—all of which required a well-maintained fire or stove (which the couple didn't have) to prepare.

"For the first three days we followed the menu," said the man. "We got up early and built our cooking fire; stopped at noon and built another. It was a hassle. By the end of the third day we had covered only 15 miles. Then the rains hit and we couldn't start a fire. So we pulled out all the dried stuff— crackers and cheese, peanut butter and jelly, etc. With no fires to slow us down, we began making time. We started averaging 15 miles a day instead of 5. Now, we're seeing the country—and that's what we came here for!"

When I offered to show the couple how to make a wet-weather fire, they politely declined, reaffirming their commitment to the joys of efficient traveling.

Admittedly, PBJs and cold cheese sandwiches are not my cup of tea, even on a fast-paced camping trip. I prefer a more middle-ground approach—a

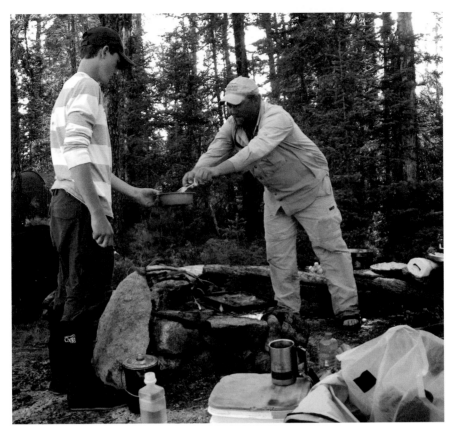

Nothing beats fresh caught fish, griddle-fried over an open fire. Note the roll of paper towels on the log. You can never have too much paper toweling on a camping trip!

reasonably quick breakfast, no-cook lunch, and a lazy but determined supper. Some of my favorite trail meals are listed below:

Easy Breakfasts

When cold granola and instant oatmeal get boring, try these delicious hot cereals:

Red River Cereal is a nutritious blend of crunchy grains that's served in the best fishing camps in Canada. It cooks to a rich creamy consistency in just five minutes. Most supermarkets have it.

Kashi is a breakfast pilaf made from seven whole grains and sesame. It's a pleasant change from traditional hot cereals.

Sturdiwheat hot cereal has a rich taste (the outer wheat layers are left on the grain). Get it from the Sturdiwheat company in Red Wing, Minnesota (see Appendix).

Old time, slow-cook oatmeal. Really, now, when did you last have the real thing?

If you want to make these cereals taste grand, add dehydrated fruit, raisins, and brown sugar to the cold water before you start cooking. For mouthwatering elegance, include chopped dates and walnuts.

No cereal is complete without milk, which you'll have to rehydrate from powdered form. Most powdered milk you find in grocery stores tastes awful. Milkman ("with the kiss of cream") is by far the best. It's available only in camping stores. Sanalac, which you'll find at specialty supermarkets, is nearly as good and much less expensive.

Lunches

Except when I operate out of a base camp, I prefer lunches that need no cooking. My meals tend to be nutritious but spartan and center around these ingredients:

Pita (Mediterranean pocket) bread—keeps at least a week without refrigeration

Assorted cheeses and hard sausage

Granola bars

Peanut butter and jelly

Wylers or Kool-Aid instant fruit drink

Hard candies

Something salty—mixed nuts, pretzels, etc.

Suppers

After two very predictable meals, supper is a blessing. Often I am quite extravagant, relying on canned sauces and fresh vegetables to spark life into the menu. Instant Lipton and Knorr soups are a traditional part of every dinner, as is some kind of dessert. If time permits, I'll bake cinnamon rolls or chocolate cake on my trail stove (see section on ovens, later in this chapter), and later contentedly pig out on popcorn and spiced tea. Otherwise, I rely on dried foods such as Minute Rice, instant mashed potatoes, noodles, and Bisquick. And for auto camping, where weight is no object, anything goes—that is, if it will fit in my 60-quart ice chest.

Go-light campers may find that one-pot meals get boring in a few days. Midway through a long trip, I serve Pita Pizza: It's everyone's favorite meal.

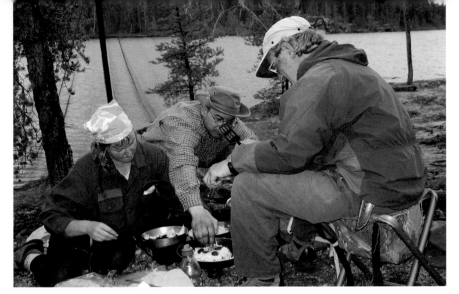

Making steam-fried pita pizza.

Pita Pizza for Four

Ingredients

Suggested toppings: pepperoni, summer sausage, hard salami, fresh
onion, black olives, canned mushrooms, anchovies, smoked oysters, etc.

½ cup dried tomato powder or one 14-ounce can of tomato paste

Spices: oregano, garlic powder, salt, cayenne pepper, basil

One or two pieces of pita bread per person

⅓ lb. fresh mozzarella cheese (vacuum-sealed cheese keeps for weeks)

Procedure

1. Slice and fry the meat and drain off the grease on paper toweling. Thickly
   dice the vegetables and mushrooms, fry them in light oil, then drain off
   the grease and set them aside.

2. To make the pizza sauce, pour the tomato powder into a bowl and add
   water to make a thick paste, or use canned tomato paste. Sprinkle on
   oregano, garlic, basil, salt, and cayenne.

3. Fry an unsliced pita at low heat in a well-oiled (I prefer olive oil), covered
   skillet. When the bottom of the pita is brown (in about twenty seconds),
   flip it over and thickly spread on tomato sauce, cheese, cooked meat, and
   toppings to taste. Immediately add a dash of water (to steam-melt the
   cheese) and cover the pan. Allow the pizza to cook at very low heat for
   half a minute, or until the cheese has melted. You'll love it.

Munchies

Car campers will prey heavily on junk foods, while hikers, bikers, and canoeists will opt for more nutritious snacks, such as fruitcake, dehydrated fruit, popcorn, granola bars, and mixed nuts. (**Note:** Cashews have the highest nutritional value of the various nuts.)

Packing Suggestions

To eliminate confusion, package each meal for your group as a complete unit. Remove all unnecessary packaging to save as much weight and space as possible. I pack flowable solids such as Tang and baking mix in small ziplock bags, which are then encased in sturdy nylon bags. Breakable and crushable items such as crackers and cheese go inside rigid cardboard containers. A cut-down cereal box works fine, but a half-gallon milk carton is ideal. Later, in camp, you can use the milk carton for mixing Kool-Aid and puddings. Or shred it up for use as an emergency fire-starter.

Each plastic-bagged meal should be placed into its own color-coded waterproof nylon sack. You'll save much pack groping at meal time if you adopt a color-coded system. I traditionally pack my breakfasts in green bags, my lunches in blue, and suppers in red. Since I don't like surprises, I label the contents of each sack on the outside with crayon.

If you pack your food in discreet, premeasured units as I suggest, everything will be at hand—and you'll never have to eat damp oatmeal.

Fresh vegetables will keep much longer on a camping trip if, before you leave home, you soak them for a few minutes in a tub (about two gallons) of water to which a quarter cup of bleach is added. This method is similar to that used to treat drinking water. Be sure your hands are clean when you remove the treated vegetables from the water. Dry the vegetables with paper toweling, then place them in a porous cotton bag. Or wrap them (separately) in a paper towel and put them in a plastic vegetable bag. Rinse the vegetables in fresh water before you use them.

Tip. Meats and vegetables will keep longer on a camping trip if you keep them cool. An "insulated" packsack like the CCS (Cooke Custom Sewing) foam-lined food pack shown on page 15 is one solution. Or, line any soft pack with a closed-cell foam sleeping pad. Procedure: Roll up the pad and set the roll upright in the pack. As the pad unrolls, it will conform to the shape of the pack's side walls. The pad will provide insulation and rigidity.

Liquids are best carried in plastic bottles that have screw-cap lids. Nalgene polyethylene containers are the most reliable. Supermarket syrup and honey bottles work marginally well if you replace their plastic pop-tops with rigid caps that won't accidentally release. Another solution is to melt the flip tops to a mass of flowable plastic in the burner of your stove.

Food Preparation Hints

Biscuits and cakes. Don't mix batter in a bowl: It's too messy. Instead, pre-measure the bake stuff into a large plastic bag. Add water to the bag, then knead its contents until the texture is right. Cut a slit in the bag bottom, then squeeze (use the bag like a cake decorator) the contents into your awaiting oven. Voilà! No mess or waste. Burn the plastic bag.

Making popcorn. Making popcorn for large groups is a hassle, even if you have a large pot. Here's an easier way: As you complete each batch of popped corn, pour it into a large paper grocery sack (don't use a plastic bag—the hot corn will melt through it!). Season the corn and shake the bag to mix. Later, burn the bag.

Paper towels. Paper toweling is always handy on a campout. If you pack a half-dozen sheets of toweling with each meal, you won't have to search for the main roll when dishwashing time rolls around.

Cookware

You can get along with about half as much cookware as you think you need. Two nesting pots, a coffee/tea pot, fry pan, plastic bowls, insulated cups, spoons, and a ladle (a stainless steel Sierra cup makes a good ladle) are enough for a party of four.

Don't waste your money on Trail Queen nested cooksets that contain useless items. Buy the pots you need and fill out the rest with materials from your kitchen. In the end you'll save weight, space, and money, and enjoy real utility.

Two covered pots, a skillet, coffee/tea pot and a ladle are all you need. A stainless steel Sierra cup makes a fine ladle.

Ovens

If you plan to bake, you'll need an oven of some sort. Polished aluminum reflector ovens are traditional but outdated in these days of small fires and trail stoves. My vote goes to the Jell-O mold oven (Figure 5-1), which is nothing more than a large-ring aluminum Jell-O mold and a high cover.

Jell-O mold ovens will work on any trail stove and will produce quality bake stuff in about the same time as your home oven.

Figure 5-1
A Jell-O mold oven.

To use the Jell-O mold for baking on your stove:

1. Grease the mold and pour your bake stuff into the outside ring. Decrease the suggested amount of water by up to one fourth for faster baking.

2. Bring the stove to its normal operating temperature, then reduce the heat to the lowest possible blue-flame setting. Center the Jell-O mold over the burner head, top it with a high cover necessary to provide sufficient room for the bake goods to rise), and relax. Cooking times are nearly identical to those suggested in the baking directions.

   Tip. "Large burner" stoves, such as the Coleman Peak 1 and double-burner models, may burn the edges of the bake stuff. An electric stove burner shield—available for a few dollars at most supermarkets—will eliminate this problem. Simply place the shield under the Jell-O mold. The air space between the shield and mold bottom will prevent burning. The large-size burner shield will fit large-ring Jell-O molds perfectly.

The double-pan method of baking on your stove is another alternative. You'll need two nesting skillets, a high cover, and a half dozen small nails or stones.

1. Scatter the nails or stones onto the surface of the large (bottom) frying pan.

2. Place your bake stuff into the small frying pan and set it on top of the nails or stones (the two pans must be separated by nails or stones to prevent burning).

3. Cover the unit and place it on your stove. Use the lowest possible blue-flame setting.

Warning. Don't use this method with a thin aluminum skillet on the bottom; you'll burn a hole right through it!

Pitfalls of Winter Cooking

Your body burns much more energy in winter than in summer, so rely heavily on foods that are rich in fat and carbohydrates (fats contain about twice as many calories per pound as carbohydrates and are the body's major source of stored energy). Unfortunately, some fat-rich foods that are summer favorites don't work well in winter. A good example is peanut butter. Try chiseling peanut butter out of a poly bottle at twenty below zero and you'll see why.

Cheese, another high-fat food, doesn't fare too well either—mainly because it tastes like candle wax when near frozen. However, cheese melts nicely into any hot food.

Salami (any sausage), on the other hand, tastes good frozen or thawed. You can use it as is or to fortify soups and freeze-dried entrees.

Food preparation tips. It takes much longer to cook foods in winter than in summer, so increase cooking times substantially. "Cook-in-the-bag" entrees such as those made by Mountain House will cook at low temperatures if you set the boiling-water–filled food bag into a covered pot of near-boiling water for ten minutes. This procedure will assure complete cooking and eliminate a dirty pot.

Since an icy wind can rob heat from a thin aluminum pot almost as fast as your stove can produce it, keep your pots covered and sheltered. A good procedure is to simply burrow the kitchen below the surface of the snow.

You may also want to make a cozy for your pots from any quilted or knitted material. A two-piece cozy (top hat and Velcro-secured band) is more versatile and energy efficient than a one-piece "teapot" model. When your food has cooked, remove the pot from the flame, set it on a square of closed-cell foam, and slip on the cozy. Use spare clothing (not nylon, which melts!) for insulation if you don't have "proper" cozies. (See Figure 5-2.)

Figure 5-2
Cozy cooking

Removable cozy cover closes with velcro

Insulated cozy band

Washing dishes. Some winter campers advise cleaning dishes with snow (a messy procedure). I've found it's better to wash them the traditional way in boiling water (no soap). I wear light wool gloves under plastic-coated cotton ones to keep my hands toasty warm and dry throughout the experience. Bacteria are inactive in frigid temperatures, so it's not necessary to rinse and dry your cookware. A little grease on your bowl won't hurt you—as long as it's your grease. It follows that each camper must have his/her own bowl, cup, and spoon.

Bowls and such. Give some thought to the selection of plastic cups and bowls. Plastic that is brittle in the store may shatter on the winter trail. Surprisingly, inexpensive, flexible plastics are often superior to stronger but more brittle, expensive ones.

Keep your cooking and eating utensils secured in a compartmented fabric roll so you won't lose them in a snowdrift. And pack spices in screw-top containers, not salt shakers, which gum up.

Cold feet. The cook spends considerable time just standing around, so some sort of insulation underfoot is essential. An 18-inch square of half-inch-thick closed-cell foam is ideal. I suggest you don't use your foam sleeping pad for this purpose, because your nighttime comfort depends on keeping it absolutely dry.

To light up your life. Winter days are short, so you may need to depend on artificial light for cooking. An LED headlamp with lithium batteries is the smart way to go. Alkaline batteries are not reliable in severe cold. ***Tip:*** keep your headlamp inside your sleeping bag at night.

To keep liquids from freezing. Liquids freeze less rapidly if they're capped and submerged in the snow. Freezing begins at the air interface of a liquid, so store beverage-filled poly bottles upside down. This way you're less apt to experience the difficulty of removing a frozen bottle cap.

A stainless-steel Thermos bottle may save more than its weight in stove fuel. I fill my Thermos as soon as the tea is done to save reheating it later. If there's a campfire, I set the Thermos near it for warmth. And when I retire, the vacuum bottle goes into the bag with me to ensure a ready hot drink come morning.

Major cooking dangers. When it's twenty below and you're dressed in a down parka and double-shell mittens, performing simple chores such as turning down the stove or lifting a pot cover takes on new dimensions. A real danger centers around use of the stove. For example, I once burned a large hole in the sleeve of an expensive down parka when I passed my arm too close to the stove burner. Subzero clothing is a good insulator, so you may not detect a burn until much of your outfit has gone up in flames. Be extremely careful around stoves when you're bundled up.

Incidentally, use care when handling stove fuels (gasoline and kerosene) in cold weather. Liquid fuels freeze at much lower temperatures than water so you're set for instant frostbite should you inadvertently spill some on bare hands. For safety's sake, handle fuel bottles while wearing gloves.

Leftovers. A major summer problem—what to do with uneaten food—is minimized in winter. I simply scoop frozen food waste into a ziplock bag and carry it along until I have the opportunity to burn it. Some winter travelers leave uneaten food on the snow for the animals—a practice not approved by national park and forest service personnel. Careless food habits—especially in winter when natural foods are scarce—might turn an ordinarily shy critter into a bold, nasty one. Wild animals are perfectly capable of finding their own dinner (in any season) without man's help.

Old hands at summer camping should have no trouble adapting to the subtle differences of the winter kitchen. The important thing is to experiment with foods and cooking procedures before you take to the winter woods.

CHAPTER 6

Expert Camping Procedures

For two days, the TV blasted warnings of the coming storm. Just south of us were 40-mile-an-hour winds and ice-cold rain. By all reports, the weather system would hit us sometime Saturday. Nonetheless, we refused to alter our plans, the rule in Scouting being "You never cancel a campout."

When we pulled into the campground, the sky was already darkening. Scoutmaster Chic Sheridan and I studied the terrain: We figured we had maybe an hour to rig a snug camp, so we went to work immediately.

There were three spots for tents: The lower level—located about 2 feet above the river—would provide room for a half dozen tents. The wide, flat terrace farther up could take four. And the gentle, rolling hill top could hold two or three.

An upward glance revealed that the hill was out of the question, as it was already occupied by a state-of-the-art nylon dome. Granted, we could probably crowd one or two Scout tents alongside, but the positioning would be only temporary: The first stormy blast would send them crashing down. No, the hill was simply a bad location.

On the lower level near the river, there was plenty of space for our five tents, but we declined the option, knowing full well the dangers of a major storm and a rising river.

"Over there," called Chic, pointing to the center terrace. "Get 'em up boys!" Now, the apparent disorder of before came to a halt. Suddenly, everyone seemed to know exactly what he was doing. Within minutes, tents were pitched and battened for the worst.

The Scout tents were primitive compared to the exotic dome on the hill—just old but solid canvas wall tents with sewn-in floors and a single vertical pole at each end. Nonetheless, we knew they'd withstand quite a blow if properly rigged.

Figure 6-1
Stormproofing the tent.

Shock-cord loop takes strain off tent fabric when storm lines are not used.

Extra storm lines added here.

Storm lines

First, the boys placed an oversize plastic groundsheet inside each tent, taking care to fold the edges of the plastic well up the sidewalls. This would protect the sleeping bags of those boys who slept along the perimeter. Next, they attached two stout guylines to each tent peak (Figure 6-1) and fanned them out to stakes below. Each tent was now held firm by three taut ropes at each end. Years before, I had installed loops of quarter-inch shock cord at the peak of each tent to absorb the stress normally reserved for the stitching and fabric.

"Run storm lines off the side, too! And weight the windward stakes with big rocks," I called. The younger Scouts followed the example of the older ones, who scampered about and barked commands. The boys meticulously tied lengths of parachute cord to the nylon loops we'd sewn to the tent hems. Now, instead of just three stakes per sidewall, there were five. The view from the hill looked like Charlotte's web. Hopefully, it would be as secure.

"Okay, boys," I shouted. "Let's get two rain flies (tarps) up. Pair 'em off a common ridge. Get on it!"

Again, the fur began to fly. First, a drum-tight rope was strung between two trees. Then two boys tied the ridge of the tarp while two more staked the tail. Coiled loops of parachute cord tied to the main face of the tarp were pulled free and staked out to nearby trees—a procedure that required less

Quick-rig tarp. Note that the leading edge is tied to a tight rope. This distributes wind-stress evenly and prevents the tarp corners from tearing in high winds. For complete protection in heavy rain, two tarps can be paired. Little Missouri River/Teddy Roosevelt National Park, North Dakota.

than three minutes. When the first fly was set, a second was mated, A-frame fashion, alongside. No need to search for extra cord or stakes—everything required was in the nylon bag that contained each tarp (see Rigging the Tarp, later in this chapter).

Ten minutes later we crowded under the low-slung flies, ready to prepare a gourmet supper and laugh at the whims of nature. I fired up the gas stove and put on the coffeepot while Chic greeted the three college kids who'd dropped in to comment on our show.

"That your dome up there?" I questioned, pointing to the hill.

"Yeah," said one of the boys proudly.

"You know you're right in the path of the storm," I quipped.

"No biggie," was the reply. "They say it'll take 50-mile-an-hour winds."

"Hope you're right; the test will come any time now."

With that, one of the boys poked gentle fun at our canvas menagerie, slyly suggesting that the wind gods would probably flatten everything by morning. I just smiled: we knew better.

Within the hour it began, innocently at first, with a light drizzle that lasted for an hour. Then the storm intensified; soon rain fell in thick sheets, driven by winds of 40 miles an hour.

Once during the night I sat up in despair and hugged the rear pole, certain the tent was about to come crashing down. But it held fast, testimony to our weatherproofing.

We awoke the following morning to the scene of disaster. There were downed trees and debris everywhere. One of our tents was partially collapsed, though the boys inside were still fast asleep. I stole a skyward glance toward the hilltop. The dome? It was gone, and so were the boys who'd occupied it. All that remained was a swatch of blue nylon tangled in branches high above.

Chic and I exchanged smug glances: we'd weathered the storm!

Let's review the procedures for effective stormproofing:

1. Always use a plastic groundcloth inside your tent. Water that wicks through worn floor fabric and/or seams will be trapped by the ground sheet. Never put the groundcloth under the tent floor.

2. Attach loops of shock cord to all guylines. Shock cords take up the wind stress normally reserved for seams and fittings. Even a badly sewn, poorly reinforced tent can be used in severe weather if it's outfitted with shock cords.

3. Know the shortcomings of your tent and correct them. Reinforce questionable seams and add additional stake loops if you need them.

4. When high winds threaten, run additional guylines off each tent peak.

Special Considerations for Stormproofing Self-supporting Tents

Most of today's tents are somewhat self-supporting, such as the Eureka! Timberline and most domes. This can be good or bad, depending on how seriously you take the "self-supporting" part. The fact is, you must stake and guy self-supporting tents or they'll blow down in big winds. It can be very entertaining to watch a cheap dome tent in a high wind—an oncoming gust flattens the tent, which seconds later springs back into shape. Unfortunately, those who are sleeping inside aren't laughing.

Domes are very comfortable tents (you can sleep in any direction), but most are poorly ventilated and questionably watertight in heavy rains. They also have lots of long poles, which must be clipped to the canopy or painstakingly threaded through sleeves. And while you're doing this, the tent—which is laying flat on the ground—is exposed to rain. You get exactly what you pay for when you buy a dome tent. Cheap domes leak in rain and blow down in wind; pricey geodesic styles, such as the Arctic-proven North Face VE 24-25, are watertight and secure in gale force winds. They are quite remarkable all-weather tents.

Use these tricks to stormproof your self-supporting tent:

1. Sew nylon "storm loops" on the face of the fly, in line with tent poles. Position loops midway down the poles as illustrated in Figure 6-2, and be sure to back what you sew with heavy material. Next, sew a Velcro tab to the inside of the fly, opposite each loop. Seal the seams you've sewn. I prefer to use Thompson's Water Seal, which you can get at any hardware store. One application with a foam varnish brush lasts for years. When a wind blows up, Velcro the loops to the poles behind them, and run a guyline from the loop to the ground. This will transfer wind stress from the nylon fly directly to the poles. You need to guy only the windward poles.

2. Double-stake your tent on soft ground; use log or rock anchors on rock (Figure 6-3). Two stakes per loop—each through a separate hole, and at a different angle—doubles the surface area and holding power in soft ground. On rock or sand, try the double stake anchor method illustrated in Figure 6-3. **Tip.** Tie 3-foot lengths of parachute cord to each stake loop before your trip, and you won't have to mess with cutting and tying these anchor lines in a rainstorm!

Figure 6-2

Stormproofing a self-supporting tent.

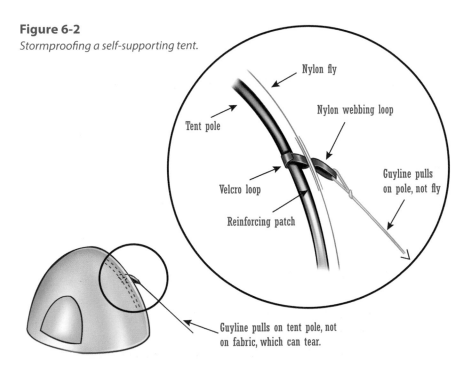

Nylon fly

Nylon webbing loop

Tent pole

Guyline pulls on pole, not fly

Velcro loop

Reinforcing patch

Guyline pulls on tent pole, not on fabric, which can tear.

Figure 6-3
Soft ground tent anchors.

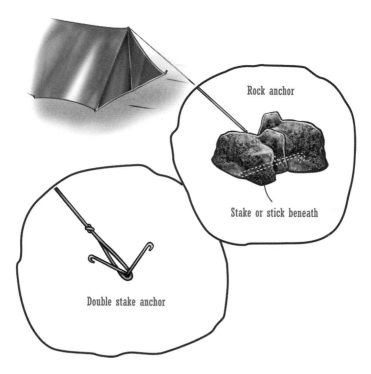

Rock anchor

Stake or stick beneath

Double stake anchor

3. Buy a vestibule for your tent if one is available: It will completely cover the poorly protected entryway and provide a place to store gear.

4. It bears repeating that you should always use a generously sized plastic groundcloth inside your tent. In winter you may put the groundcloth under your tent to keep the tent floor from freezing to the ground.

Rigging the Tarp

Stormproofing your tent is only half the solution to keeping dry in rain. The other part is having a dry place to cook and relax. A large (10 foot by 12 foot) nylon tarp pitched between trees or suspended from guyed poles will provide ample protection for four.

For a quick rainproof shelter that won't flap in the wind, try this rigging procedure:

1. String a tight line about 6 feet high between two trees. Use two half-hitches at one end of the rope and a power-cinch with a quick-release knot at the other (see Chapter 7 for a review of knots and hitches).

2. Tie one edge of the fly to the line. This will distribute the wind load among several points along the fly. Wrap the corner ties around the line a few times before you tie them to produce friction so the fly won't slide inward along the line when it's buffeted by wind.

3. Stake down the back end of the fly, then guy the center to an overhanging limb or rope strung overhead. If this is impossible, prop out the center from the inside with a pole. Don't try this unless you've sewn a protective pole patch to the fly. Without one, you'll stretch the fly out of shape or tear it. And don't use Visklamps (ball and garter devices) to pitch a fly. Visklamps stretch and abrade fabric unmercifully.

   If the center pole falls down in high winds, the fly will collapse. To secure the pole to the fly, sew two opposing "butterfly pole" loops to the inside of the fly, as illustrated in Figure 6-5. Thread a piece of parachute

Figure 6-4
To customize the rain tarp, add ties to all the grommets and sew five equally spaced loops to the face. This will allow you to pitch the tarp in a variety of geometric configurations.

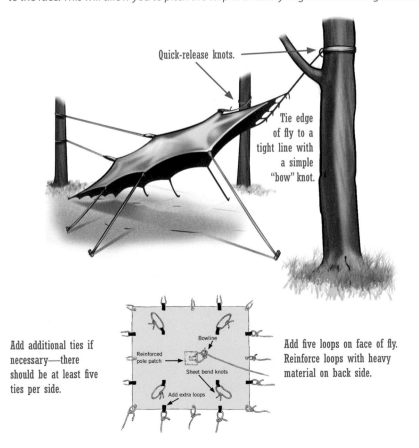

Quick-release knots.

Tie edge of fly to a tight line with a simple "bow" knot.

Add additional ties if necessary—there should be at least five ties per side.

Bowline

Reinforced pole patch

Sheet bend knots

Add extra loops

Add five loops on face of fly. Reinforce loops with heavy material on back side.

Figure 6-5

To secure the pole to the fly, sew two opposing "butterfly pole" loops to the inside of the fly.

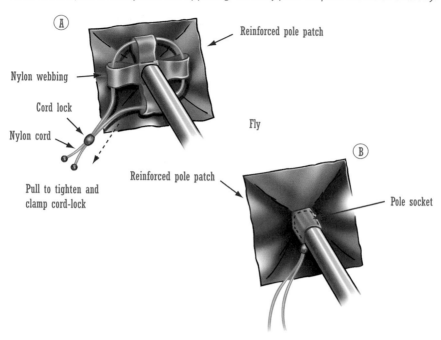

(A)

Reinforced pole patch

Nylon webbing

Cord lock

Nylon cord

Fly

(B)

Reinforced pole patch

Pole socket

Pull to tighten and
clamp cord-lock

cord through the loops and secure the cords with a nylon cord lock. Now
your center pole will stay put in high winds.

To use the "butterfly pole" loops, center the pole in the "socket" and
tighten the cord lock. The loops will wrap around the pole and hold it in
place when the tarp is buffeted by wind. For extra security, wrap the cords
around the pole a few times and tie them with a simple bow.

4. Guy the sides as the terrain permits. Be sure you complete all knots and
    hitches with quick-release loops, as explained in Chapter 7, so you can
    change or drop the outfit at a moment's notice. When severe winds
    threaten, simply lower one or both ends of the ridge rope.

Packing the fly. Pack your fly in a nylon bag, along with about 100 feet of
parachute cord (cut into 10–15-foot lengths) and eight tempered aluminum
tent stakes. This will greatly simplify pitching.

For large groups, pair two tarps at the ridge. Overlap one tarp so there'll
be no leaks.

A snug camp. Adirondack Park, New York.

Snug Camp

Campcraft books are rich with advice on choosing the right campsite. But most commentary is a waste of space, since even a rank novice knows better than to pitch his tent in a depression, on unlevel ground, or in a bog. Since it's unethical (and often illegal) to clear trees and brush and to "improve" sites by trenching around tents, you usually have to take what's available and make the best of it. Forest Service and Park personnel don't always establish campsites with an eye for the lay of the land. Most of the time, I'm overjoyed just to find a level place to set my tent. After that I worry about creature comforts such as a south-facing slope, proximity to good water, effective drainage, shade and wind protection, a nice view, etc.

Nonetheless, here's one bit of advice worth repeating: Don't camp in a meadow or flat mossy area. Cold, damp air settles in meadows, and moss acts like a giant sponge: It traps water for miles around. If it rains while you're camped on moss, you'll be elbow-deep in water by morning. Even the most watertight groundcloth won't save you under these conditions.

Bears

There are two views about bears: One suggests that all bruins are timid and will run at the first smell of you. The other warns that bears are mankillers and advises you to bring big guns.

Between these extremes is the real truth. Most bears are timid and will ordinarily stay away from humans. But bears can be ornery, like some people. Many bears start each new day looking for a meal; if you come upon a recent kill or get between a sow and her cubs, you've got big problems. Research by Stephen Herrero and James Gary Shelton suggest that people may have more to fear from bears than was previously thought. If you're intrigued by bears, read the books *Bear Attacks, Their Causes and Avoidance*, by Stephen Herrero (Lyons Press, 2002); *Bear Encounter Survival Guide*, by James Gary Shelton (James Gary Shelton, 1994); and *Bear Attacks: The Deadly Truth*, by James Gary Shelton (James Gary Shelton, 1998). I suggest you read these books in the order in which they are listed.

Protecting Your Food Supply

Don't store food inside your car. Bears are experts at getting into cars. They'll insert their claws through the tiniest openings in windows and doors and rip out the glass or metal to get at food.

Use a critter-proof container. A plastic or metal ice chest will deter squirrels and rodents. A thick-walled PVC plastic pipe with threaded end caps will

This bad boy came into the author's camp right at supper time (smart bear!). Note the tent in the foreground and the sleeping bag airing on the line. Along the Fond du Lac River, Saskatchewan, Canada. Rob Kesselring

The Outsak (left) is made from stainless steel. It is squirrel and raccoon-proof, but not bear-proof. It is shown here with an Aloksak odorproof bag inside. Right: The Ursak which is woven from Kevlar®, is bear-proof!

stop bears. There are some commercial bear-proof containers but they are heavy and bulky. The Ursak (ursack.com), a lightweight bag woven from Kevlar®, is the exception. It is reliably bear-proof and approved for use in most national parks. Important! Seal your food in an Opsak (loksak.com) odorproof bag before you place it into the Ursak. If small varmints are your main concern, the Outsak (simpleoutdoorstore.com), which is made from stainless steel netting, is all you need. It will stop squirrels and raccoons but not bears. If you want to know which animal-resistant products work best, check with the managers of national parks that have a large bear population, such as Yellowstone and Glacier.

Don't hang your food in a tree. Expert campers usually do not store their food in trees. Instead, they seal their food tightly in plastic to eliminate odors (I suggest vacuum sealing), then they remove the food from the immediate camp area. Setting food packs outside the campsite perimeter is usually enough to foil hungry bruins and other animals. Rationale: Bears are creatures of habit—they quickly learn that camps, packs, and tin cans contain food. In each campsite there are only a few trees with limbs high enough to deter a bruin. Bears aren't stupid; they learn the location of these trees and make daily rounds to secure whatever is suspended from them. When they find something (anything) hanging from "their" tree, they'll get it down, one way or another. All black bears (even fat old sows) can climb to some degree. And cubs shinny like monkeys. James Gary Shelton has discovered that, contrary to popular belief, grizzlies can "hook" climb with their legs, just like humans. The point is that, if momma can't get your food, the kids will! Polar bears are the only bears that absolutely, positively don't climb.

Recommendation. Double-bag (in plastic) all foodstuffs, especially meats. Ask your grocer to vacuum-seal smelly foods. Or, use odor-proof plastic bags. Set food packs on low ground (to minimize the travel of odors) well away from the confines of campsites and trails. As an added precaution, separate food packs by 50 feet or more. Do not, as commonly advised, put food packs in trees.

If you're camping in grizzly country, locate your kitchen at least 50 yards downwind of your tents. Naturally, cooking areas must be scrupulously clean—free of even the last Rice Krispy. Nonetheless, human odor is stronger than most food smells: Don't be surprised if the bear smells you before he smells your food.

Bear Encounters

Here are the recommended procedures in the event you meet a bear face to face.

Black Bears

Blackies are timid and will ordinarily run away at the first smell of you. Bears don't see very well; what most people interpret as a "charge" is usually nothing more than simple curiosity. Screaming, blowing whistles, and other noise-making will usually send a wild bear running, but an experienced camp bear will remain totally oblivious to the racket. The best procedure is to hold your ground, spread your arms wide (so you look bigger), talk authoritatively, and back off slowly. Do not run.

The danger signs are "woofing and clacking." If the bear goes "woof, woof, woof," and you hear loud hiccuping sounds with the clacking of teeth, the situation is deteriorating. The bear's mad and unpredictable. If there's a tree handy, climb it now. If you can beat a path to safer ground, go for it. If you are attacked, fight like mad. Do not play dead with a black bear.

Pepper spray (sometimes called "bear mace") contains 10 percent oleo capsicum, the flaming ingredient in red pepper. If properly used it will stop bears about 75 percent of the time. Herrero did not find a single case where spraying a bear with pepper enraged it and made it more aggressive.

Don't spray your camp to keep bears away. While bears don't like to be sprayed with pepper, they do like the taste of it. Evidently, bears like spicy food, too.

There are a number of formulations of "bear mace." I rely on Counter Assault. It's available on the Web at counterassault.com. You'll want the one-pound can. A quick-draw holster is a must.

Grizzlies

Grizzlies are shy animals and will usually run away from you. The grizzly is the king of the hill in its domain, so it's doubtful you can bluff one. I was once charged by three grizzlies on the open tundra of Canada, and I can vouch for the effectiveness of this procedure:

1. Talk in a moderate, non-threatening tone to the bear as you slowly back away. Do not make eye contact. Let the bear know that you made a mistake and are trying to skedaddle.

2. If the bear runs toward you, interpret this as curiosity, not a charge. Remember, bears can't smell you if you're downwind.

3. When the bear is within 50 feet, drop to the ground, face down, nose in the dirt, and clasp your hands tightly behind your head. Spread your legs wide so the bear can't turn you over easily. ***Note:*** Until recently, the recommended method was to assume a tight fetal position, hands behind the head. I did this, and it worked for me. Discouraging bears is not an exact science.

Stephen Herrero, author of *Bear Attacks*, suggests that the face-down plan is best. Herrero found that the face is where most serious injury occurs. If the bear bites and claws you, try to remain quiet and passive. If the bear tries to flip you over, do a complete roll and maintain the face-down position. You will probably survive the attack.

Insects

Everyone knows that repellents are essential on most camping trips. But the color of your clothes is also important. Insects (especially mosquitoes) are attracted to dark colors, notably navy blue. Powder-blue, yellow, white, and most greens and reds are neutral. If you're camping with children, choose a mild cream repellent rather than a more effective one which is high in DEET (N-N Diethyl-metatoluamide). Strong repellents may burn sensitive young skin. Keep repellents away from plastics: These products will instantly dissolve eyeglasses, polypropylene underwear, and the handles of Swiss Army knives.

Bugs are attracted to dark colors, notably navy blue and black. Note that nearly all the bugs on the light blue pack are on the navy blue straps.

Headnets are essential for early season trips in the northern states and Canada. You can make a headnet in a few minutes. Just sew up a wide rectangle of mosquito net, large enough to fit over your head and wide-brimmed hat, and long enough to drape on your shoulders.

It's difficult to see through milk-colored netting. If you can't find a dark-colored headnet, buy a light-colored one and darken the eye panel with black felt-tipped pen, dye, or spray paint.

Bug jackets range from simple netted jackets (that bugs can bite through but can't fly through) to the sophisticated Original Bug Shirt (bugshirt.com), which has an integral hood and zippered headnet. A breathable nylon jacket and headnet works about as well—but is hotter to wear. There are also mesh jackets that you soak with DEET (which is allowed to dry). The repellent discourages insects and the cool mesh keeps them away from your body. I prefer this type.

Some Final Tips

1. Bugs will avoid your face if you saturate your bandanna with repellent and tie it loosely around your neck. Spray the underside of your hat brim, too.

2. Some of the most effective first-aid products for bug bites contain aloe, a plant-derived ingredient that has been around for thousands of years. Aloe soothes inflammation, inhibits swelling, and keeps skin moist. It also soothes burns and kills bacteria and fungi. To be effective, aloe should make up at least 80 percent of the product's formula.

3. If you are concerned about using a DEET-based repellent, try this: First, apply a bonding-base sunscreen to your skin. Wait several minutes, then apply repellent over the sunscreen. The sunscreen will keep the DEET from being absorbed into your skin.

4. Use a lotion or cream on your skin and a spray on your clothing. Liquid or cream repellents are more potent (a better buy) than sprays.

5. Household ammonia and water will cut the sting of mosquito bites. For bee, wasp, and hornet stings, apply a wet salt pack and allow it to dry. The salt will draw the pain away quickly.

Susie Bug Net

First, you apply DEET to all exposed skin. As more insects hone in, you add a headnet, then a bug jacket. Ultimately, you rant and swear, then in disgust retire to your insect-proof tent. Meanwhile, friends nearby enjoy a bug-free after-dinner brandy and a glorious sunset inside their "Susie bug net"— personal-size bug armor designed by my wife, Sue Harings.

Materials needed: A piece of mosquito netting 60 to 72 inches wide and 8 feet long, plus enough ⅛-inch diameter shock cord to span the hem. Don't use no-see-um net: It's not strong enough, and you can't see through it.

Procedure: Fold the netting lengthwise to produce a rectangular sheet that measures about 8 feet by 6 feet. Sew up the two long sides, hem the bottom, and install the bungee cord in the hem. The finished net will weigh less than a pound and compress to football size.

Sue Harings, the author's wife, models the "Susie bug net" she designed. When bugs are bad, you can even take it swimming!

Here are some uses for your Susie bug net:

1. Eat inside it; there's room for two.

2. Sleep out under the stars. The net covers you from head to toe. Remember to cinch the bungee cord tightly around the foot of your sleeping bag.

3. Use as a "portable outhouse" when bugs are bad.

4. Bathe in it! Amble to the beach as a ghostly apparition in your Susie bug net. Wear your life vest and you'll float confidently inside your bug armor.

5. Lay the net over breads, cheese, and lunch meats to keep flies away.

6. Rig a tripod inside and you have a tiny bug-proof tepee in which to wash dishes, cook, and make repairs.

Roll and stuff your Susie bug net under a pack flap, so it will be available at meals and river rest stops.

Note. You can buy a Susie bug net from Cooke Custom Sewing, Inc. (cookecustomsewing.com).

Ecological Concerns

Food leftovers should be bagged in plastic and packed out of the woods. When this is impractical, the best method of disposal is burning. Even soupy foodstuffs will burn if you add them a little at a time to a hot fire.

Burn all garbage completely, being sure to pick aluminum foil out of the flames. Burn out tin cans and flatten them with the back of your handaxe or rock, and pack them out. Fish entrails should not be thrown into a waterway, where they will increase bacteria levels and reduce the supply of oxygen for fish. Instead, bury viscera 4 to 8 inches deep, as far as possible from the campsite. This relatively shallow depth is best for decomposition and also minimizes the possibility of it being dug up by animals. If there's only an inch or two of soil cover available, weight remains with a heavy rock or log.

Important! Be wary of packing out garbage when hiking in grizzly country. You *must* eliminate the faintest odor or you risk a bear attack. If in doubt, burn your leftovers or bury them *far* from camp and hiking trails, or toss them into a nearby river, where they will be consumed by fish and microorganisms.

Human waste should be buried 4 to 8 inches deep too (an aluminum tube with one end flattened makes a good shovel). Toilet paper and sanitary napkins should be burned, because these items require a full year or more to degrade. And please don't throw food (or anything else) in Forest Service box latrines or chemical toilets. Bears commonly upset latrines to get at food. The mess that results is indescribable.

Note: Some national parks require that human waste be carried out. Most disposable toilet systems are heavy, bulky, and require some set-up. I recommend Biffy Bags (biffybag.com). They are lightweight, compact, and inexpensive. Biffy Bags are the only human waste disposal system I've used that remain odor-free for up to a week.

Dishes should be washed 100 feet away from a water source. Greasy dishwater is best poured into a small hole in the ground and covered with a few inches of soil. It should go without saying that you should never bathe (with soap) in any waterway.

Water Purification

If you value your health, you'll get your drinking water only from approved sources, or you'll treat it or carry it with you.

I confess to laziness in this respect. I despise the taste of chemically treated water; I don't like to mess with filters, and at eight pounds per gallon, I'll seldom carry more than a canteen full of water. Usually, I obtain my drinking water from a lake or river, though I'm very careful where I get it. Here are the guidelines I religiously follow:

1. Go well away from any shoreline to get drinking water. If you're camping at a spot that is frequented by man or animals, go upstream of the source to get your water. On lakes, a minimum of 100 feet from shore is recommended—and the farther out you go, the better.

2. Decay organisms (bacteria, protozoans, and fungi) generally prefer the shallows, so the deeper your water source, the better.

3. Avoid any water with a greenish tinge. It contains algae and is usually loaded with microorganisms.

4. Don't take water from backwaters and stagnant areas. These are breeding places for microorganisms.

5. Don't drink any water that has been contaminated by wastes from a paper mill. Secure your water from incoming streams instead.

6. Don't take water near beaver dams or lodges. Beaver are the favored host of Giardia lamblia—a small protozoan that will make you plenty sick. The disease (called Giardiasis) is characterized by severe diarrhea, cramps, nausea, gas, and vomiting. Incubation time is generally one or two weeks, though some people have gone as long as two months without

developing symptoms. If untreated, Giardiasis may go on for years. The disease is not at all easy to diagnose.

Field Methods of Water Treatment

Boiling
Boiling will kill almost everything, even Giardia and Cryptosporidium, which can survive long exposure to iodine and chlorine. The EPA recommends a one minute rolling boil for elevations under 2,000 meters (6,600 feet) and three minutes for higher elevations.

Filters
Filters strain out microorganisms, but they don't kill them. The critters are just trapped and held inside the filter. Eventually, the filter loads up (water flow decreases), and you have to clean or replace it. Filter pore size is the nemesis of all filtration units. Pores small enough to trap the tiniest microbes impede water flow and pumping efficiency; large pores let more water through—and possibly some dangerous germs too! Filters may have pumps or be gravity-fed. Gravity-fed units are bulky but they're as effective as pumps and more trouble-free. They're great if you need to filter a lot of water fast and don't want to labor with a pump.

Purifiers and Purifier Filters
Purifiers kill microorganisms (including viruses) but they don't remove them. Purifier/filters trap *and* kill them. Purifier/filters have smaller pores than filters and thus a slower rate of flow. Relatively new are water bottles with built-in purifier/filters. Just fill the bottle with water and drink up. Some even have straws!

Ultraviolet Purifiers
People with lake homes have long relied on ultraviolet light to kill microorganisms. The popular SteriPen®—a Magic-Marker sized purifier that operates on small batteries—was among the first to use this technology. Just insert the UV bulb into a water bottle and activate the light. When the light turns off (in about a minute) the water is safe to drink. UV purifiers will destroy Giardia, Cryptosporidium, and viruses. But they won't remove sediment or work in cloudy water. And they can only purify small amounts (usually 1 liter or less) of water at a time.

Chemical Treatment

Water-treatment tablets are safe and easy to use. However, they will not reliably kill Cryptosporidium which, fortunately, is uncommon in surface waters. Boiling is the best way to destroy Cryptosporidium cysts. Be aware that water-treatment tablets require time to work—at least thirty minutes if the water temperature is above 68°F. Much longer for cold or cloudy water. Important: Tablets lose potency over time—fresh ones work faster. *Tip:* To reduce the bitter taste after treatment, aerate your water (pour it back and forth between two canteens).

Removing Silt

Desert rivers like the Colorado, Green, and Missouri are too silty to drink. If you try to filter out the silt, your filter will quickly clog. Here's an easy way to remove the silt.

Procedure:

1. Fill a 2-gallon bucket with the silty water and add about a teaspoon (the amount isn't critical) of alum to it. Alum is used in home pickling to add crispness and as a settling agent in water treatment plants. It is nontoxic and tasteless. Most pharmacies have it. A 12-ounce (340 gram) bottle contains enough alum to settle about 24 gallons of silty water.

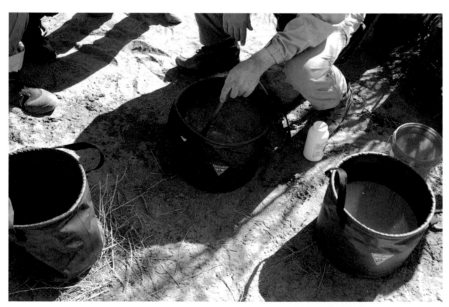

Settling silt with alum. Left: stirring alum into the silty water. Right: Twenty minutes later—the silt has settled. Use a ladle to draw off the clear effluent on top. Note the bottle of alum between the two buckets.

2. Very *slowly* stir the water in *one direction* only. Continue stirring until a snowlike precipitate forms in the water—it takes about five minutes.

3. STOP stirring. Allow the water to settle for about 20 minutes. At the end of this time, the water will be clear and the silt will have settled to the bottom.

4. Gently dip the clear effluent from the top of the bucket then filter or chemically treat the water to make it potable.

CHAPTER 7

Ropemanship

Given enough rope—and time—anyone can rig a snug camp. Add a knife, and anyone can cut one down. Between these extremes are a small number of elite outdoorspeople who can match the right knot to the job at hand—and untie it instantly the morning after an all-night rain. Stroll through a wooded campground at season's end and count the number of tightly knotted cords you see hanging hopelessly from the vegetation and you'll understand the importance of ropemanship.

Outdoor handbooks define dozens of knots, most of which are quite useless in the woods. In reality, all you need to know are two knots and two hitches. Learn these well and you'll be at home in any situation, even those that require some rescue work.

Old-timers will note the conspicuous absence of the square knot and tautline hitch. Except for limited first-aid applications, the square knot is worthless; and the infamous tautline hitch—so useful in the days of cotton tents and manila rope—has now been replaced by the much more powerful and versatile power cinch.

The Double Half-Hitch (Two Half-Hitches)

The double half-hitch (Figure 7-1) is useful for tying a rope to a tree, as for a clothesline or to rig a tarp. The knot is very secure and tends to tighten itself when a load is applied. If you want to get this knot out quickly, finish it with a quick-release loop as shown in Figure 7-6.

Figure 7-1

Double half-hitch

The Sheet Bend

Figure 7-2
Sheet bend

Use the sheet bend for tying two ropes together. The knot works well even when rope sizes are dissimilar. The sheet bend is about the only knot that can be used to join the ends of slippery polypropylene rope.

A friend once won five dollars when he fixed a broken water-ski towrope with this knot. When the towline snapped, the owner of the ski boat bet my friend he couldn't tie the two ends of the slick polypropylene rope together tightly enough to hold. No problem. My friend won the bet and skied the remainder of the day on the repaired line.

It's important that the free ends of the sheet bend be on the same side, as shown in Figure 7-2. The knot will work if the ends are opposite, but it will be less secure.

The Bowline

Figure 7-3
Bowline

Here's an absolutely secure knot that won't slip regardless of the load applied. The bowline is the most important knot for mountain climbing. Use it whenever you want to put a nonslip loop on the end of a line or around your waist.

Beginners are often told to make the bowline by forming a loop, or "rabbit hole." The rabbit (free end of the rope) comes up through the hole, around the tree (opposite or long end of the rope shown in Figure 7-3) and back down the hole. The knot will slip a few inches before it tightens, so allow an extra-long free end.

Power Cinch (aka Trucker's Hitch)

This ingenious hitch (Figure 7-4) works like a winch with a 2:1 mechanical advantage. Use it to secure the lines of a tent to a stake or tree (Figure 7-5) or to rig a drum-tight clothesline in camp. The power cinch is the hitch of choice whenever you need a secure tie-down. Carrying canoes on car tops, lashing furniture into the bed of pickup trucks, and tying tents and sleeping bags to aluminum pack frames are all useful applications of this versatile hitch.

Begin the power cinch by forming the loop shown in Figure 7-4, step 1. Pull the loop through as in step 2. It's important that the loop be formed exactly as shown. The loop will look okay if you make it backwards, but it won't work.

If the loop is formed as in step 2, a simple tug on the rope will eliminate it. This is preferable to the common practice of tying a knot in the loop, which, after being exposed to a load, is almost impossible to get out.

If you're tying a load in place on top of a car, tie one end of the rope to the load and snap the steel hook on the other end of the rope to the car's bumper—or, if you're using a car-top carrier, run the rope from bar to bar, using two half-hitches on one side and a power cinch on the other. Run the free end of the rope (a) through the loop in the power cinch (step 2), and apply power to the free end. You've created a pulley with a 2:1 mechanical advantage.

Complete the hitch by securing a double half-hitch around the body of the rope, or use a quick-release loop as illustrated.

Figure 7-4
Power cinch

- ① Form overhead loop — Standing end — Working end
- ② Pull loop through — Pull tight — Tied to canoe or object
- ③ Pull
- ④ Standing part
- Standing part — Working end — Tight loop — Insert working end through loop and pull

Figure 7-5
*Secure your tent to a tree
stake with a power cinch.*

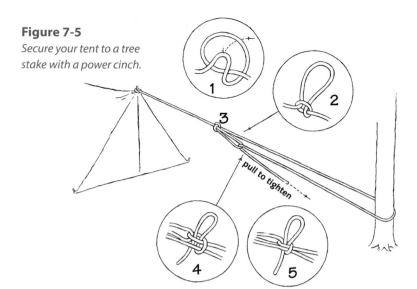

1
2
3

pull to tighten

4
5

The Quick-Release Loop

There's nothing more frustrating than untying a bunch of tight knots when you're breaking camp in the morning. If you end your knots with a quick-release loop like that illustrated in Figure 7-6, you'll be able to untie your lines with a single pull.

Form the quick-release feature by running the free end of the rope back through the completed knot—the same as making a "bow" when tying your shoes.

Use a simple overhand knot with a quick-release loop to seal the stuff sacks that contain your sleeping bag and personal gear (Figure 7-6). The plastic cord-locks sold for this purpose are for people who don't know how to tie effective quick-release knots.

Figure 7-6
*Secure your stuff sacks with
a quick-release loop.*

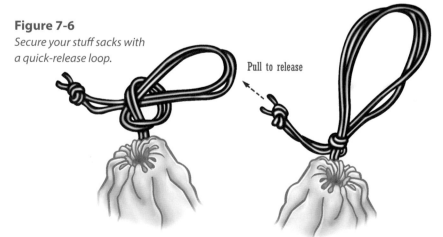

Pull to release

CHAPTER 8

Dangers

Everyone has heard grim tales about campers who have been lost in the woods, struck by lightning, crushed by a fallen tree, or drowned while swimming.

People who don't camp out react with horror to these stories and solemnly agree that the wild outdoors must be very dangerous. Experienced campers know better. In fact, most experienced outdoorspeople travel the bush for years without ever having an accident. There are occasional challenges, to be sure, but death-defying encounters are rare. Competent campers respect nature and have a proven battle plan to escape its dangers. They also have the skills to execute their plan.

Herein lies the secret of safe outdoor travel: Have the skills to carry out your battle plan!

Here are some common camping concerns.

Sprained Ankle

For years I got by with adhesive tape and an Ace bandage. Then my doctor gave me a lightweight air splint, which works much better. I've found that a person can walk confidently within minutes after spraining an ankle if he or she wears an air cast. Bring an air cast if you're going in harm's way.

Object in the Eye

Some years ago a woman in my canoeing class got sand beneath her contact lenses when her canoe capsized. The pain was unbearable. I gently lifted each eyelid and flushed out the particles with generous quantities of Eye Stream, a sterile irrigation solution. Then, I applied a ribbon of Polysporin ophthalmic ointment (Yellow oxide of mercury, ophthalmic 2 percent is the non-prescription alternative) inside each lower lid and immobilized the eyes with oval eye patches and microfoam tape. Finally, I administered Tylenol.

The woman said the pain ceased shortly after I applied the ointment. The next day she called to report that her doctor was so pleased with the treatment that he simply applied more ointment and replaced the bandages. Naturally, I was thrilled I had done things right.

Of all the medications in my kit, Polysporin ophthalmic ointment and large, oval eye patches have been most useful. I've used these several times to treat eye infections and scratched corneas.

Tip. Eye patches are also great for patching blisters.

Hypothermia—Killer of the Unprepared

The morning begins with a golden sun; by noon scattered clouds of twisted gray appear low on the horizon. Within the hour an icy drizzle falls. Curious, you look skyward, hopeful the discomfort will soon pass. But it doesn't. The rain continues. You snug the hood of your well-worn rain parka in hopes of discouraging the chilling drizzle, which has already soaked your cotton T-shirt and blue jeans. Soon, you begin to shiver, slightly at first, then uncontrollably. Ultimately, your speech thickens and you lose orientation. It's hard now to tell up from down, right from left. One minute you're walking drone-like down the muddy trail, the next, you're on your knees groping.

Total collapse comes an hour later. Suddenly, your sense of feel and awareness is gone. Shivering ceases, muscles become rigid; the once tender, pink skin becomes puffy white. You have penetrated the danger zone. Without help, you'll drift further into oblivion, toward death—the final goal.

Fortunately, knowledgeable friends are nearby and in command. Within minutes a tent is pitched and foam pads and bedding are placed inside. Wet clothes are stripped from your inanimate body and you are rushed to the awaiting sleeping bag where you are sandwiched—skin to skin—between two friends. Additional sleeping bags and parkas are pulled from their stuff sacks and piled over you. Nearby, someone struggles with a trail stove—hot soup is on the way.

The condition persists for many minutes, but ultimately your frigid body is rewarmed and you are able to sit up and talk intelligently. Now that you can swallow, you are given gentle sips of hot broth and are cheered back to your former state.

You are very lucky. Without such well-directed, quick assistance, you surely would have died!

In the old days, they called it "exposure sickness." Now the technical term is *hypothermia*. But the cause—and symptoms—are the same. Hypothermia is a lowering of the body's core temperature. It may result from being plunged into cold water (immersion hypothermia), or from slow chilling, as in the above example.

The onset of hypothermia occurs when body temperature drops below about 95 degrees Fahrenheit. As blood is rushed to the vital organs, chilling spreads throughout the body. This is accompanied by clumsiness, slurred speech, and loss of judgment. Coma and death may occur within a few hours if the body temperature is not raised.

Most hypothermics are unaware of what is happening to them and will maintain an "I'm okay" attitude to the bitter end. It's up to other members of the party to observe the signals and take appropriate action.

Treatment for hypothermia consists of removing wet clothes and sandwiching the victim between two people in a sleeping bag, `a la the illustrative example. Radiant heat from a fire may be used to speed the warming process, and is probably the quickest way to warm a hypothermic under typical field conditions. Be careful, though: intense heat may burn the sensitive skin of the victim.

Hypothermia is physically and emotionally draining. Victims should be allowed to rest for a full day following the experience.

Your best protection against hypothermia is prevention. Select reliable rain gear and choose clothing that insulates well when wet. Wool is the traditional fabric, although polypropylene and fleece work as well. Wet cotton literally wicks heat from the skin, so this fabric should never be worn in tricky weather. As mentioned, blue jeans are the worst thing you can wear in the backcountry.

Finally, keep the calories flowing while you hike. Constant nibbling on candy/nuts/granola, etc. will keep the temperature of your "furnace" high. If you get wet, stop immediately and change clothes. Many have died from hypothermia while clinging to the belief that they were saving their dry clothes for camp.

Lightning

The risk of being struck by lightning may be sharply reduced if you religiously follow these guidelines:

1. Lightning usually strikes the highest object in its path, so if you pitch your tent in an open field, be certain there are trees or rock formations of significantly greater height nearby.

2. A cone of protection extends from the tallest trees or landmass (as the case may be) about 45 degrees outward. Stay within this cone of protection, but far enough from its source so that lightning can't jump from the object to you. Lightning may jump a dozen feet or more from the base of a tree, so don't crowd tall trees too closely. (See Figure 8-1.)

Figure 8-1
Stay within the cone of protection, but not so close that lightning may jump from the tree to you.

45°

3. Lightning may travel along the roots of trees, which may extend dozens of feet outward. If roots are close to the surface of the ground, as in rocky areas where there is little soil cover, sufficient energy may be transmitted along subsurface roots to pose a danger to anyone standing on the ground above them. Keep this in mind when you pitch your tent!

4. If you're caught outside the cone of protection and suddenly feel electrical energy building (dry hair will stand on end), immediately get as low as possible to reduce the human lightning-rod effect.

5. If you're in a tent and lightning strikes all around, sit up immediately and draw your legs to your chest so that only your buttocks and feet touch the ground. A foam sleeping pad (preferably doubled) placed beneath you may provide enough insulation to keep you from being grounded.

You must maintain the recommended "sitting" position during an electrical storm. In the unlikely event you are struck by lightning while in this position, only your feet and buttocks are apt to burn. But if you're lying flat, the electricity may stop your heart!

After the Strike!

Lightning usually kills people by stopping their heart. It may also paralyze the respiratory system. If your friend has been struck by lightning—and is alive—the burns are probably minor and you can attend to them later. The important thing is to begin CPR immediately and get the heart going again.

Electrocution may cause disorientation, coma, seizures, and spinal cord injuries. It may also rupture the eardrums. All you can do until help arrives is to keep your friend immobilized and warm and convince him that he'll be okay.

Widow Makers

Always check your campsite for tall leaning trees, especially dead or damaged ones, which may come crashing down on you in a windstorm. Old-time woodsmen call these leaning trees "widow makers." Can you guess why?

Some tree species are weaker than others. Watch out for soft maples (silver maple and box elder), which can split violently, and stands of young trees that are not protected from wind by bigger trees. Also, be wary of big old trees whose roots run very close to the surface of the ground.

Swimming

Swimming and camping trips naturally go together. But, please wear shoes of some sort when you take to water. The toughest feet are no match for rusty tin cans and broken bottles.

Chopping with an Axe

An axe can slip or glance. For this reason, I recommend the safe splitting procedure illustrated on page 24. Use a saw—not an axe—to cut wood to length. Then use your axe and the two-handed method to split the wood.

Forest Fires

As forester in Oregon many years ago, I fought several forest fires. Here's what to do if you're camping and see a forest fire heading your way:

Try to outflank the blaze by moving perpendicular to its path. If possible, stay on or near water. If there's a nearby lake, go into it and stay there. Wet down your clothes and hat. Remove all nylon and polypropylene clothing— these synthetics produce terrible burns. ***Note:*** Intense heat can turn the water in wet clothes to steam, which will burn you badly. Wet down your clothes only if there's water nearby where you can cool off.

If sparks are flying and you have a boat, capsize the boat and get under it for protection. The air bubble trapped inside will enable you to breathe.

Winds generally drive fires uphill. Move downhill if you can; seek out a valley to rest or camp. Fires usually die down at night and flare up with the morning winds, so evening through dawn is the best time to travel.

Fires may jump half a mile or more—so being near a large body of water won't make you safe!

Forest Fire! Along the Porcupine River, Saskatchewan, Canada. This fire was less than a mile from our camp. Fortunately, it didn't jump to our side of the lake.

Getting Lost

Most beginning campers secretly admit a deep fear of getting lost in the woods and not being found. In truth, if you carry a knife and matches or a butane lighter on all your outings, and can make a one-match fire (see chapter 3), you have little to fear. If you do get lost, stay put and build a huge, smoky bonfire. Searchers will find you in a matter of hours or days.

It would be unfair to leave the subject of navigation without mentioning the wonderful GPS (global positioning system) units that are on the market. These battery-powered units receive signals from twenty-four orbiting satellites. With a civilian model GPS, you can locate your position (within 10 meters) anywhere on earth in a matter of minutes—if you can read a map, that is!

Compass and GPS. To use a GPS effectively, you must first know how to read a map and compass. This compass is an Orienteering model. Orienteering compasses have a built-in protractor that allows you to determine a bearing (heading) off a map without orienting the map to north. And when the bearing is set on the dial, it remains locked there until you change it.

Outdoorspeople are buying GPS units like mad, though precious few know how to use them. To use a GPS effectively, you must first know how to read a map and compass. And, your maps must have a coordinate system that the GPS unit can understand. Not all maps do.

If you're serious about learning the GPS system, first learn how to use a map and compass. My book, *Basic Illustrated: Map & Compass*, will get you started right.

Manufacturer and Product Information

Biffy Bag
(651) 206-3078
biffybag.com
Personal disposal toilet system in a bag. Lightweight, compact, and long-term odor-free.

Cooke Custom Sewing, Inc.
(651) 784-8777
cookecustomsewing.com
Great packs, rain tarps, canoe covers, and more. I'm proud to say I've had a hand in some of the designs.

Duluth Pack
(800) 777-4439
duluthpack.com
Traditional canvas packs, Ullfrotte wool long underwear, Grohmann knives, Gransfors Bruks axes, and more.

Eagle's Nest Outfitters, Inc.
(828) 252-7808
eaglesnestoutfittersinc.com
Trail-proven hammocks for casual use and serious camping.

Fast Bucksaw, Inc.
(651) 437-2566
fastbucksaw.com
Best folding camp saw I've found. Expect to wait weeks for delivery.

Frost River

(800) 375–9394

frostriver.com

Traditionally styled McAllister waxed canvas packs, bags, briefcases, tents, tarps, and more.

Gränsfors Bruks, Inc.

(800) 433-2863

fax: (803) 821-2285

gransfors.com

Best axes on the planet. Hand-forged, superbly balanced, and razor sharp.

Idaho Knife Works

(509) 994-9394

idahoknifeworks.com

Source of the "Cliff" knife I designed and other terrific outdoors knives by Mike Mann.

Littlbug Enterprises, Inc.

(763) 684-0141

littlbug.com

The Littlbug wood-burning stove is lightweight, compact, and powerful.

Loksak Waterproof Bags

(435) 649-9009

fax: (435) 940-0956

loksak.com

These bags look and function like ziplock bags but they're stronger and more reliable. Used by the military and adventure-racing teams to protect maps, GPS units, and satellite phones. Aloksak also makes odor-proof (OP) plastic bags that are also waterproof.

Original Bug Shirt Company

(800) 998-9096

bugshirt.com

Most popular bug shirt.

Piragis Northwoods Company

(800) 223-6565

piragis.com

Hard-to-find high-tech gear, as well as my 2002 video *The Forgotten Skills*, which presents the most important skills that are detailed in this book.

Sturdiwheat

(800) 201-9650

sturdiwheat.com

Best pancake mix I've found. Just add water.

Index

About the Author

Cliff Jacobson is a professional canoe outfitter and guide, a wilderness canoeing and camping consultant, and the author of more than a dozen top-selling books on camping and canoeing. His video, *The Forgotten Skills*, details the most important campcraft procedures.

Cliff's unique methods are proven by the sweat of pack and paddle and are reminiscent of the days when skills were more important than things. Cliff has developed many popular educational materials that are widely used in schools. His Wilderness Meal activity, which teaches wilderness ethics (detailed in his book, *Boundary Waters Canoe Camping*), has been called "the most successful environmental activity of all time." Cliff also wrote the Minnesota State map and compass (orienteering) curriculum for Minnesota schools, and a popular water quality curriculum (*Water Water Everywhere*, published by the HACH Co.) that is used nationwide.

Cliff is a retired eighth-grade environmental science teacher who now splits his time between canoeing and camping, and sharing his love for the sport by writing and teaching about it. When he's not writing, speaking, or leading canoe trips in northern Canada, he's out paddling his solo canoe or figuring out a new way to improve his equipment.

In 2003, the American Canoe Association presented Cliff with the Legends of Paddling award and inducted him into the ACA Hall of Fame.

8/16